Building
YOUR OUTDOOR HOME

30 EASY LANDSCAPING PROJECTS

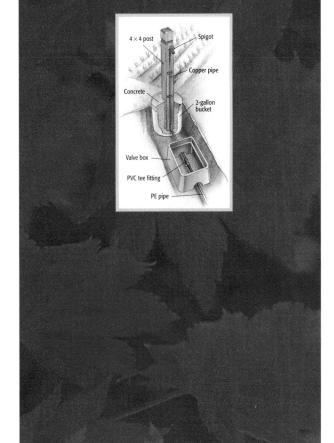

CREATIVE
PUBLISHING
international

MINNETONKA, MINNESOTA

Credits

Executive Editor: Bryan Trandem
Associate Creative Director: Tim Himsel
Art Directors: Kari Johnston & Gina Seeling
Managing Editor: Jennifer Caliandro
Project Manager: Michelle Skudlarek
Author: Christian Paschke
Editor: Jerri Farris
Technical Production Editors:
  Keith Thompson, Philip Schmidt
Technical Photo Editors:
  Scott Christensen, Tom Heck,
  Joel Schmarje
Copy Editor: Janice Cauley'
Mac Designers: Patricia Goar, Jonathan Hinz,
  Jon Simpson, Brad Webster
Vice President of Photography & Production:
  Jim Bindas
Studio Services Manager: Marcia Chambers
Photo Services Coordinator: Carol Osterhus
Photographers: Tate Carlson, Jamey Mauk,
  Andrea Rugg, Rebecca Schmitt
Photographer Assistants: Greg Wallace,
  Keven Timian
Cover Photography: Jamey Mauk
Scene Shop Carpenters: Troy Johnson,
  Dan Widerski
Manager, Production Services: Kim Gerber
Production Manager: Stasia Dorn
Illustrators: Jan-Willem Boer, Rich Stromwall

CREATIVE PUBLISHING international

Copyright© 1999
Creative Publishing international, Inc.
5900 Green Oak Drive
Minnetonka, MN 55343
1-800-328-3895
All rights reserved
Printed by R. R. Donnelley & Sons Co.

President: Iain Macfarlane
Group Director, Book Development: Zoe Graul
Director, Creative Development: Lisa Rosenthal
Executive Managing Editor: Elaine Perry

Created by: The Editors of Creative
Publishing international, Inc. in
cooperation with Black & Decker.
BLACK&DECKER is a trademark of the
Black & Decker Corporation and
is used under license.

Library of Congress Cataloging-in-Publication Data

Building your outdoor home :
30 easy landscaping projects.
      p.   cm. -- (Black & Decker outdoor home)
    Includes index.
    ISBN 0-86573-339-2 (hardcover)
    ISBN 0-86573-756-8 (softcover)
1. Garden structures--Design and construction--
Amateurs' manuals. 2. Landscape construction--
Amateurs' manuals. 3. Landscape gardening--
Amateurs' manuals. I. Creative Publishing
International. II. Series.
TH4961.B85 1999
635.9--dc21   98-49605

Contents

BUILDING YOUR OUTDOOR HOME

Welcome

Whether you're reading this book to explore possibilities and gather information, or have a complete set of landscape plans in hand, you've probably been dreaming about a new landscape for quite some time. And you know that most landscape construction doesn't produce instant gratification.

In fact, building a new landscape is a lot like embarking on a journey—it requires vision, planning, faith in yourself, and some hard work. And, as with any journey of substance, there may be moments when you wonder what you were thinking when you decided to venture into new territory. But with proper preparation and a little advice from good sources, you'll find that building a new outdoor home for yourself and your family is not only entirely possible, it's fun and tremendously rewarding.

If you're almost ready to begin construction, you already have a clear idea of what you want to build. What you really need is background information, construction tips and techniques, and step-by-step instructions for the projects you're planning. *Building*

If you haven't already designed a landscape plan, you'll need to draft one before you begin construction. One option is to hire a landscape designer or architect. But with a little research, you can create a professional-quality plan yourself. There are many books available on the subject of landscape design. Black & Decker's *Designing Your Outdoor Home* is one; it presents a thorough but down-to-earth look at designing outdoor rooms and landscape plans.

Your Outdoor Home presents 30 do-it-yourself projects designed to help you accomplish your goals, whether you're starting a new landscape from scratch or renovating an existing one.

This book provides information and suggestions that bring a variety of landscape projects within reach of enthusiastic do-it-yourselfers. If you're experienced, most of the projects will be easy to follow. If you're just beginning to discover the joys of doing it yourself, some may seem a little intimidating. Don't worry; just start with the simpler elements in your landscape plan. You'll gain confidence and acquire new skills each time you tackle a project. Before you know it, you'll be ready for anything.

Many of the projects can be completed in one weekend, using tools you probably already own. Others require more time, rented tools or machinery, or specific skills. Some of the plumbing and electrical utilities projects, for instance, require basic plumbing and wiring skills. If you're not experienced in these areas, you can learn about basic plumbing and electrical techniques from home improvement books, such as Black & Decker's *Complete Guide to Home Plumbing* and *Complete Guide to Home Wiring*.

As you get ready to break ground, we encourage you to relax and enjoy yourself. When possible, invite family and friends to help you with these projects. Take photographs of yourselves and the work in progress, and keep a scrapbook. You'll be building memories right along with landscape elements that you'll proudly use and enjoy for years to come.

About This Book

Building *Your Outdoor Home* contains all the background information and how-to techniques you'll need to build a complete landscape from start to finish. But deciding where to start can be difficult. To help guide you, we've divided the book into seven sections that follow the chronology of the landscaping process. This process is the same one that professional landscapers follow: gathering information, shaping the landscape, installing utilities, building walls and ceilings, creating landscape floors and adding landscape accents.

Whether you plan to landscape your entire yard all at once, or complete the work in sections over a longer period of time, following this process will make the job more efficient. Here's a brief overview of the sections covering the stages of the landscaping process:

Basics covers all of the information you'll need to gather and consider before you begin the landscaping projects in this book. The information presented here will help you select and shop for materials, plants and tools. There's also a detailed guide to soil analysis and a look at the details that must be cleared with neighbors and officials before you begin landscaping your yard.

Shaping outlines the steps for creating a solid foundation for landscape projects. This section demonstrates how to alter the shape of your yard by demolishing existing elements, grading the soil, adding steps, building a retaining wall and creating a berm. In addition to managing and creating slope, you'll find several projects for solving common drainage problems.

Utilities features projects for adding plumbing and electrical amenities to your yard, such as a sprinkler system and low-voltage landscape lighting.

Walls & Ceilings demonstrates methods for creating living and nonliving landscape walls and ceilings, including fences, hedges, stone walls, trees and arbors.

Floors contains projects for creating a variety of attractive landscape floors. Among the projects in this section, you'll find methods for building simple pathways, paved patios and walkways from brick and stone, versatile decks and lush, healthy lawns.

Accents shows you how to add the finishing touches to your outdoor rooms. The gardening projects show you how to build garden areas, raised timber beds and container gardens. Other projects demonstrate easy, practical solutions for furnishing outdoor rooms. You'll also find all the information you'll need to create an enchanting garden pond complete with plants, fish and a fountain.

Basics

Creating a well-conceived landscape plan is the first step to building your outdoor home. But there's more to forming a landscape plan than drawing a detailed map of your new yard. The planning process also involves gathering information, making decisions and handling the logistical details that must be resolved before you begin to dig or build.

Early in the planning process, you'll need to decide what materials you're going to use to create the new landscape elements in your yard. For hardscape projects, such as landscape walls and floors, consider the look, durability and prices of available materials. With softscape features, such as hedges and garden beds, select plants that grow well in your climate and in the conditions of your yard. Once you've decided on materials, the next step is to determine quantities and locate suppliers.

Gathering the necessary tools is also part of the planning process. You probably already have many of the basic tools you'll need, but you may lack some of the more specialized tools. You'll probably need to rent some tools to complete certain projects, and locating and reserving them ahead of time will help you avoid frustration.

Researching local Building Codes and requirements, applying for work permits and checking with your neighbors allows you to make any necessary changes to your landscape plan before you begin working. Skipping this step can have unfortunate consequences, ranging from paying expensive fines to starting a project over from scratch.

Before you complete the planning, have your soil analyzed. Make sure to leave plenty of time for this step, as it takes anywhere from three to six weeks to get the results. The soil test report you receive will tell you how to amend your soil before you begin planting.

IN THIS CHAPTER:

Materials

Wood, natural stone and manufactured stone are the primary materials for building landscape elements. Metal and plastics are secondary materials, used in the hardware you'll need for many projects, and for installing plumbing and electrical amenities.

WOOD

Home supply centers and lumberyards carry a variety of lumber and other wood landscape products. Cedar, redwood, cypress and pressure-treated pine are the best options for building outdoor structures because they are resistant to moisture and insect damage. Although these woods are outdoor-grade, they do require a coating of a high-quality wood sealer/preservative every two years to maintain the durability of the wood.

NATURAL STONE

Stone quarries, home supply centers and aggregate suppliers sell a large variety of natural stone in a range of sizes and shapes for different applications. *Cut stone*, also called ashlar, is used for creating walls, pathways and walkways.

Flagstone is uncut stone that's naturally flat. It is frequently used for creating durable walkways, steps and patios.

Gravel is sold in two forms, rough and smooth, and is sorted by size. Rough gravel is used as a loose-fill material for paving floors and paths, and also for creating drainage features. Seeding aggregate, a smooth gravel, is used to texturize poured concrete. Compactible, or Class 5, gravel is commonly used as a base beneath paved surfaces.

Sand is another form of natural stone, commonly used for creating a mortarless bed for brick and stone, as well as floors in play areas.

Wood, stone, manufactured stone, plastic and metal materials are all used in landscape construction. These materials are often nonreturnable, so estimate the quantities you'll need before you buy.

Electrical and plumbing features, such as outdoor lighting and sprinkler systems, are constructed with metal and plastic materials.

MANUFACTURED STONE

A variety of concrete products are available in a wide range of sizes, textures and colors.

Poured concrete can have a smooth finish, but it can also be given a textured finish or even tinted.

Interlocking block is made from molded concrete that's designed to resemble natural stone. It's used for building retaining walls and raised garden beds.

Concrete pavers are made from poured concrete and are available in many shapes, colors and textures. Concrete brick pavers are frequently used in place of clay bricks for building patios, walkways and edging.

METAL

Metal hardware is required for many landscaping projects. Metals used outdoors must be strong and resistant to corrosion.

Connectors, such as nails, screws, post anchors and latches should be made from galvanized steel or another corrosion-resistant material.

Electrical materials include conduit, receptacle boxes and lighting fixtures. Choose materials that are outdoor-grade: galvanized thick-wall conduit, and receptacle boxes with a grounding terminal and watertight seals.

Plumbing materials, such as valves, pipes, pipe straps and spigots, are commonly made of copper or steel. Select Code-approved materials: pipes for outdoor use should be a classified as thick wall.

TIP:

To protect your yard, place a tarp for sand, gravel or other materials as close to the work area as possible.

PLASTICS

Plastic hardware is commonly used for utilities, fixtures and edging.

Electrical hardware made from plastic includes plastic-coated electrical cable, receptacles, indoor receptacle and switch boxes and light fixtures.

Plumbing materials, including PVC pipe, PE (polyethylene pipe), valve boxes and sprinkler heads are made with high-grade plastics. PVC schedule 40 piping is used for underground plumbing lines, such as sprinkler system lines.

Flexible plastic edging is an inexpensive, easy-to-install edging material. For best results, buy a professional-grade edging that's been shipped and stored flat, rather than the less durable, coiled edging often sold at home centers.

ESTIMATING MATERIALS

The chart below can help you estimate the quantities of stone and masonry materials you'll need for landscape projects. Sizes and weights of materials may vary, so consult your supplier for exact specifications.

ESTIMATING STONE & MASONRY MATERIALS:

Sand, gravel, topsoil	Surface area (sq. ft): 100 = (2" layer) = tons needed
Standard brick pavers	Surface area (sq. ft) $\times$ 5 (4" $\times$ 8") = number of pavers needed
Poured concrete	Surface area (sq. ft.) $\times$ .012 (4" layer) = cubic yards needed
Flagstone	Surface area (sq. ft.): 100 = tons of stone needed
Interlocking block	Area of wall face (sq. ft.) $\times$ 1.5 (6" $\times$ 16" face) = number of stones needed
Cut stone	Area of wall face (sq. ft.): 2-ft.-thick walls = tons of stone needed

Plants

Plants add year-round color and texture to your landscape. Determining which plants are suited to the climate in your region and to the sun and soil conditions of your planting areas is an important part of developing your landscape plan. The information here will help you select healthy specimens of the best annuals, perennials and bulbs for your yard. Similar information on shrubs and trees can be found in "Hedges" (page 64) and "Trees" (page 66).

SUPPLIERS

In most cases, you'll find the best selection of plants at nurseries and garden centers. But, if you know what to look for, you can often find good deals on plants sold at discount retailers and mail-order catalogs. When ordering plants by mail, choose a supplier that has a guaranteed return or exchange policy.

ZONE RATINGS

The U.S. Department of Agriculture (USDA) zone map is designed to help you select appropriate plants for your climate (see page 13). The zones are numbered from 1-11, based on the average annual minimum temperature of each area. If you're buying plants locally, you'll find that nurseries and garden centers typically carry only plants suited to the zone in which they're located. If you're buying plants by mail, consult plant descriptions and the zone map to make sure the plants you select are suited to your area.

ANNUALS

Annuals complete their life cycle in one season. They grow much faster than perennials, but don't survive the winter. They're usually sold in small containers packed into large trays, or "bedding flats." Healthy annuals are compact, have plenty of buds and show good leaf color and root structure. Don't buy annuals with light-colored leaves, gangly stems or roots protruding from the container.

(left) Nurseries, garden centers and home supply stores carry a selection of annuals, perennials, shrubs and trees. Selection, price and quality of merchandise are factors to consider when deciding where to shop.

(opposite) Consult the United States Department of Agriculture zone map to choose specimens suited to your climate.

PERENNIALS

Perennials return each year, growing and spreading without having to be replanted. They usually are sold as container-grown plants. Good perennials have balanced foliage, sturdy flower stalks and firm roots. Avoid perennials with sparse growth, poorly defined flower stems, shriveled or pale leaves or mushy stems.

BULBS

Bulbs are unique perennials that grow from fleshy underground root or stem structures that store the necessary nutrients for plant development. They are usually packaged in bags or sold in bulk. Healthy bulbs are large, firm and plump. Don't choose withered, dried-out bulbs or those with visible spots of disease, insect damage or decay. In general, bulbs sold in net bags, or packaged in straw or peat moss to absorb moisture, are of better quality than those packaged in plastic.

Selecting healthy plants for your landscape is easy if you pay attention to a few visual clues. Healthy perennials and annuals (right) have a compact shape with lots of buds. Poor specimens (left) may have gangly stems and exposed roots.

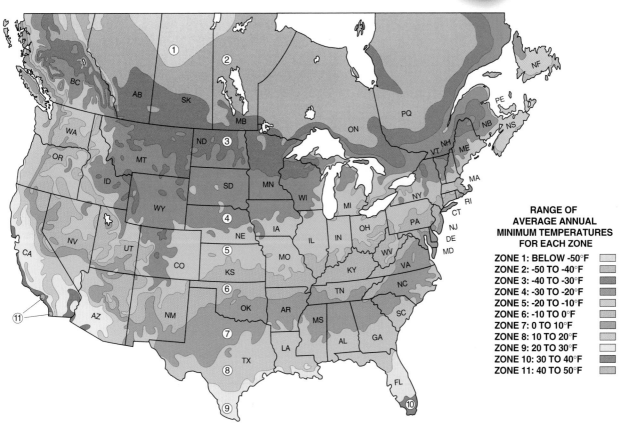

RANGE OF AVERAGE ANNUAL MINIMUM TEMPERATURES FOR EACH ZONE

ZONE 1: BELOW -50°F
ZONE 2: -50 TO -40°F
ZONE 3: -40 TO -30°F
ZONE 4: -30 TO -20°F
ZONE 5: -20 TO -10°F
ZONE 6: -10 TO 0°F
ZONE 7: 0 TO 10°F
ZONE 8: 10 TO 20°F
ZONE 9: 20 TO 30°F
ZONE 10: 30 TO 40°F
ZONE 11: 40 TO 50°F

Leaves

Grass

Peat moss

Compost

Straw

Manure

Soil

In addition to creating the foundation for your entire landscape, your soil provides the water and nutrients your plants, lawn, trees and shrubs need to develop large, healthy root systems. Very few yards, however, are blessed with perfect soil that provides an ideal growing environment. You'll probably need to amend your soil to improve its structure and nutrient levels. Whenever possible, amend the soil early in the landscaping process, when the task is easier and yields better results.

REQUESTING A SOIL TEST

To get the most accurate assessment of how to improve your soil, have it analyzed by a soil testing lab. For a small fee, a local lab or your state's agricultural extension service will conduct a detailed analysis of a soil sample from your yard.

In general, it takes anywhere from three to six weeks to receive the results of a soil analysis, so send the samples long before you plan to begin landscaping. Include written information with the sample, detailing what you've added to your soil in the past—such as fertilizers, lime, peat moss or compost. Also, include information on the specific plants you want to grow. The lab will provide a report that suggests specific amendments to add to your soil to support the plants you'll be growing.

HOW TO COLLECT A SOIL SAMPLE

For each area where you intend to plant, dig a 1-ft.-deep hole, using a clean shovel. Cut a ½"-wide slice from the top to the bottom of the hole, using the shovel. Remove the top ½" off of the slice, and place the remaining portion in a clean bucket. Repeat this process in at least five

Nitrogen is necessary for developing healthy leaf and stem growth.

Organic amendments are the best choice for improving the structure and nutrient levels of your soil.

Soil that's been amended properly has a structure that promotes a healthy root system. The roots of these annuals are deep and spread apart.

Recommendations for lawn growth tell you how to improve your soil to support a lawn.

Recommendations for vegetable and flower gardens specify how to amend the soil to foster successful gardens.

different areas of the planting site, mixing each of the slices together in the bucket.

Pour about one pint of the sample soil into a clean container, such as a locking plastic bag. Mail the sample and the written information to the soil testing lab.

HOW TO READ A SOIL TEST REPORT

The soil test report details your soil's texture, pH and nutrient levels. It will also tell you how to improve the soil in order to grow the plants you want.

Texture. Soil texture is categorized as loamy, sandy, silty, clayey or a combination of two of these categories, such as loamy-sand or silty-clay. *Loamy* soil is ideal for growing plants—it is composed of almost equal amounts of sand, silt and clay. Because sandy soil doesn't retain water or nutrients, plants must be frequently watered and fertilized. *Silty* soil holds moisture and nutrients fairly well. However, it cannot absorb a lot of water at once and requires frequent, light waterings. *Clayey* soil holds moisture and nutrients

well, but is too dense for root growth and too damp for plants that require well-drained soil.

The soil test report will suggest organic amendments, such as compost, manure or peat moss, to improve sandy, silty and clayey soils. In sandy and silty soils, organic material helps retain moisture for plant roots. In clayey soils, amendments help loosen the soil, improving breathability and drainage.

Soil pH is a value of the soil's acidity or alkalinity based on a scale from 0 to 14.0. The report will identify your soil's pH, and tell you the ideal pH for growing the plants you specified. If your soil is very acidic or alkaline, you may need to alter your plant selection.

Fertility is a measure of the quantity of nitrogen, phosphorus and potassium in the soil. The report will measure the presence of each element in parts per million (ppm), and rate each measurement as low, medium or high.

Specific recommendations. Amending poor soils with organic materials boosts nutrient levels and improves the soil's structure. The results of your soil test will suggest how you can amend your soil to foster lawn and plant growth. For detailed how-to demonstrations on applying amendments, see "Soil Preparation" (page 88). The process for amending soil for planting beds differs slightly and is covered in "Garden Beds" (page 100).

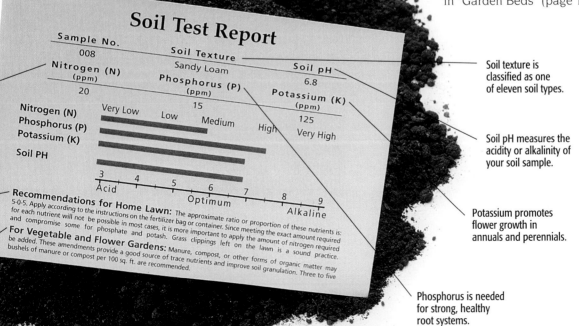

Soil Test Report

Sample No.

008

Nitrogen (N) (ppm)

20

Phosphorus (P) (ppm)

15

Soil Texture

Sandy Loam

Soil pH

6.8

Potassium (K) (ppm)

125

	Very Low	Low	Medium	High	Very High
Nitrogen (N)					
Phosphorus (P)					
Potassium (K)					

Soil PH

3   4   5   6   7   8   9
Acid   Optimum   Alkaline

Recommendations for Home Lawn: 5-0-5. Apply according to the instructions on the fertilizer bag or container. The approximate ratio or proportion of these nutrients is: for each nutrient will not be possible in most cases, it is more important to apply the amount of nitrogen required and compromise some for phosphate and potash. Grass clippings left on the lawn is a sound practice.

For Vegetable and Flower Gardens: Manure, compost, or other forms of organic matter may be added. These amendments provide a good source of trace nutrients and improve soil granulation. Three to five bushels of manure or compost per 100 sq. ft. are recommended.

Soil texture is classified as one of eleven soil types.

Soil pH measures the acidity or alkalinity of your soil sample.

Potassium promotes flower growth in annuals and perennials.

Phosphorus is needed for strong, healthy root systems.

Tools

You probably already own many of the garden and household tools needed to complete the projects presented in this book. But, several projects require more specialized tools and machinery, which may be available at rental centers. You can also borrow tools from neighbors or friends. Whenever you rent or borrow tools, ask for a copy of the owner's manual and operating instructions as well.

If you buy new tools, invest in high-quality products whenever possible. Most hardware stores and home centers carry a wide variety of hand and power tools, in a range of prices. Read consumer publications and talk to experienced do-it-yourselfers to get information about dependable brands and useful features. To ensure your safety and prevent damage to your tools, always use a GFCI (ground-fault circuit-interrupter) extension cord when using power tools.

BASIC TOOLS:

- Hammer
- Maul
- Rubber mallet
- Power drill
- Screwdriver
- Hacksaw

- Carpenter's level
- Tape measure
- Garden shovel
- Trenching spade
- Wheelbarrow
- Garden hose

- Pressure sprayer
- Garden hoe
- Trowel
- Garden rake

SPECIALTY TOOLS:

- Reciprocating saw
- Jig saw
- Chain saw
- Circular saw
- Plate compactor

- Jackhammer
- Hand tamp
- Core aerator
- Vertical mower
- Power auger

- Fish tape
- Wire combination tool
- Line level
- Framing square
- Wood float

Buy the best quality tools you can afford. A quality tool can last a lifetime, which costs less in the long run than replacing a cheaper version three or four times.

To protect your investment, keep tools clean, dry and sharpened as necessary. Protect metal tools from rust by giving them a light coat of oil from time to time.

Courtesies & Codes

Before you begin building landscape structures, communicate your plans to neighbors, building inspectors and utility companies. Although it may seem inconvenient, making these calls gives you a chance to gather information and make any necessary adjustments to your landscape plans before work begins.

NEIGHBORS

Talk with your neighbors about your landscaping plans—this simple courtesy can prevent problems ranging from soured relationships to legal disputes. Show them sketches of your plan or pictures similar to the projects you're planning, especially projects that will affect their yards, such as building fences, walls, hedges or planting large shade trees.

An inexpensive line level is indispensable for many landscaping projects.

BUILDING CODES & REGULATIONS

Determine what your community's regulations and codes are before you begin landscaping. Many communities have standards that limit the dimensions and materials for landscape structures. Check local Building Code to determine the setback distance, a regulation that prohibits any structure from being built too close to property lines. If you're adding any structures that require concrete footings, such as fences, arbors or decks, check local Building Code to determine the depth required for the footings.

UTILITY LINES

Before beginning any project that involves digging or excavation, you must locate the buried utility lines in your yard. Your electric, telephone, gas, cable and water companies are required by law to inspect your site on request and mark the locations of buried lines. Call these companies several days before you plan to start digging.

BUILDING PERMITS & INSPECTIONS

You may need to obtain building permits and schedule inspections for some of the plumbing and electrical projects in this book. To obtain permits, you'll need to submit a drawing of the project for your local building inspector to approve. The inspector will tell you if there are specific materials you'll need to use for the project and suggest any necessary changes to your plan. Once you've received your permit, you'll need to display it in a front window of your home until the project has been completed.

Shaping

The topography of your yard—its shape, contour and the position of its natural features—is a fundamental element of your landscape. The basic shape of the land affects how you use your yard, its drainage patterns and the quality of its soil, as well as the amount of work involved in routine maintenance.

As you begin building your outdoor home, you may need to alter the shape of your landscape to make it more functional. Before tackling shaping projects, you'll need to become familiar with the basics of the process: demolition, grading, managing and creating slope and solving and preventing drainage problems.

In an established yard, you may need to remove elements to make space for new outdoor rooms and landscape features. Following professional techniques makes it easier to remove existing hardscape and softscape features, such as fences, patios, walkways, hedges and trees.

If water collects near your foundation or you have other drainage problems, you probably need to address issues of slope before you begin building the features of your outdoor home. By following some simple grading techniques, you can create slopes that direct water away from your house and eliminate soggy areas in your yard. In some cases, you may choose to install a dry well or create a drainage swale to channel and disperse excess water.

Steep slopes, or no slope at all, can present practical and aesthetic challenges that often can be managed by reshaping a yard's contours. Retaining walls can prevent erosion, simplify mowing and provide level planting space in areas that were previously unusable. Adding a berm can increase privacy, muffle sound and create visual interest.

Shaping projects often are simple, but they do involve quite a bit of physical labor. Although many people enjoy doing the work themselves, others prefer to hire a landscape contractor to help with part or all of it. Rented tools and equipment can make some jobs easier, as you'll see in many of the project descriptions that follow.

IN THIS CHAPTER:

Shaping

Demolition

The shaping process often involves relocating or removing landscape elements such as fences, walls, walkways or patios to make way for the new elements in your plan. Before you begin, develop a demolition plan, outlining what you're going to remove and what tools you'll need. With careful planning, you should be able to complete all the projects that require rental tools in one lease period.

You can also save money by using the materials from demolished structures in new projects. For instance, you can use sand-set paver bricks as garden edging (page 101), broken pieces of concrete to build a freestanding garden wall (page 62) or fence posts for creating raised garden beds (page 102).

Before you begin demolition, make plans for disposing of material that can't be reused. The solution may be as simple as renting a dumpster, or it may involve hiring a disposal contractor.

The following information outlines the tools and techniques you can use to remove wood, brick, stone and concrete structures from your landscape.

To dismantle a fence that was assembled with nails, use a crowbar to pry the boards loose. After removing a board, hammer the exposed ends of the nails down against the board to prevent injury.

WOOD

Wood structures are among the simplest landscaping features to dismantle. The tools you'll need will depend on the structure and how it's built. You can dismantle decks and fences assembled with screws by removing the screws with a reversible drill or power screwdriver. For structures built with nails, use a crowbar to pry the individual boards loose. If you're not planning to reuse the lumber and can dispose of it in large sections, you might want to hire someone with a front-end loader to knock down an entire fence.

Removing the concrete footings used to anchor fence or deck posts can be a difficult task. Most footings are at least 18" deep—digging them up requires a lot of time and effort. In most cases, it's more practical to bury footings than to remove them. To bury a footing, remove 3" to 4" of the concrete surrounding the post, using a sledgehammer or a mason's hammer and chisel. Use a reciprocating saw to cut the post off flush with the remaining concrete, then cover the footing with soil.

CONCRETE

The best way to remove small concrete structures, such as a step or walkway, is to break the concrete into small sections. If you're removing a walkway, you can easily accomplish this task with a 2 × 4 and a sledgehammer. Wedge the 2 × 4 under the edge of the concrete and pry it up. Strike the elevated portion of the concrete with the sledgehammer, splitting the concrete into large pieces.

Concrete patios and driveways are more difficult to remove. The easiest method for breaking up these structures involves using a rented jackhammer. You can also use a sledgehammer to break apart the concrete, but it's a time-consuming and labor-intensive job. When renting a jackhammer, ask the rental supplier to demonstrate the proper techniques for using the tool. Wear protective clothing, safety glasses and ear protection while operating a jackhammer.

BRICK & STONE

To remove dry- or sand-set brick and stone, all you'll need is a crowbar and some patience. On pathways and patios, simply pry up the bricks or stones. If you're using a crowbar to dismantle a dry-laid stone wall, start at the top of the wall and work down, carefully prying out each stone. If you're planning to reuse the material, discard any pieces that are crumbling or cracked.

To remove mortared walkways and patios, use either a jackhammer or a sledgehammer, following the same methods described above for removing concrete. This is, of course, very hard work, and you may want to enlist volunteers or hire helpers.

An easy way to demolish a mortared wall is to knock it over with a front-end loader. If you aren't comfortable operating such an intimidating piece of equipment, hire a contractor for the job. If that's not practical, use a sledgehammer and a wedge to break off sections of the wall. Starting at the top, force the wedge into a crack or joint, then strike it with the sledgehammer. When you reach the bottom of the wall, bury the foundation.

A. Mason's hammer
B. Sledgehammer
C. Wedge D. Crowbar

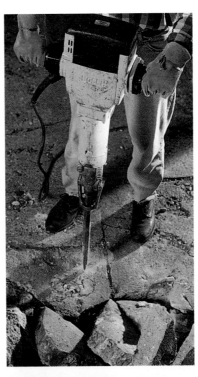

Using a jackhammer is the easiest method for demolishing concrete patios and driveways.

Pry up the edge of a walkway with a 2 × 4, then use a sledge-hammer to break the concrete into manageable pieces.

Shaping

Shrub & Tree Removal

Removing existing shrubs and trees is often a necessary part of the shaping process. Many times, shrubs and trees need to be removed to make way for new landscape features. It's also common to remove diseased or dying specimens to improve the appearance of the landscape.

Healthy shrubs and young trees (less than four years old) can sometimes be dug up and transplanted to another area of your yard. However, some species don't react well to being moved. Before you attempt to transplant a shrub or tree, check with your local nursery or extension service to make sure that moving the plant won't hinder its growth.

TOOLS & MATERIALS

- Basic tools (page 16)
- Hardhat
- Safety glasses
- Ear protection
- Bow saw
- Chain saw
- Wedge

HOW TO REMOVE SHRUBS & YOUNG TREES

If you're going to transplant a shrub or young tree, it's best to dig it up in the early spring when the plant is dormant. In order for the transplant to be successful, keep as much of the root ball intact as possible. Dig around the base of the tree, making a hole roughly the same diameter as the span of the branches. If the plant has a shallow root system, dig to a depth of 12"; plants with deeper roots require a depth of 18" to 24". To plant a transplanted shrub or tree, see the information on planting in "Hedges" (page 64) and "Trees" (page 66).

The simplest method for removing a shrub or young tree is to dig it up, using the same technique you'd use for transplanting. You can also cut it off at the base of the trunk, then dig up the stump.

HOW TO REMOVE MATURE TREES

If you need to remove a mature tree from your yard, one option is to have a tree contractor cut it down. If the tree is very large and located close to a house or building, this is the only good option. But if you're confident in your ability to use a chain saw and the

Hinge

Notch

Felling cut

A. Use a bow saw to remove all of the limbs below head-level.

B. Remove a notch, then make a felling cut, leaving a 3" hinge in the center.

tree has plenty of clearance space, you can save money by removing it yourself.

The first step in cutting down a tree is determining where you want it to fall. This area, called the *felling path*, should be roughly twice as long as the height of the tree and clear of any obstacles. You'll also need to plan two *retreat paths*, located diagonally away from the felling path. The retreat paths allow you to run away from the tree if it begins to fall in the wrong direction.

To guide the tree along the felling path, a series of cuts are made in the trunk. The first cut, called the *notch*, is made by removing a triangle-shaped section of the trunk on the side of the tree facing the felling path. A *felling cut* is then made on the opposite side, forming a wide *hinge* that guides the fall of the tree.

The following sequence outlines the steps professionals follow to fell a tree and cut it into sections. Before you begin, put on protective clothing, gloves, safety glasses, ear protection and a hard hat.

Step A: Remove Low Branches
Use a bow saw to remove any branches below head-level. Starting from the bottom of each branch, make a shallow cut up toward the center, then cut down from the top until the branch breaks away.

Step B: Make the Notch & Felling Cut
1. Using the chain saw, cut at a 45° angle, about ⅓ of the way into the trunk. **Do not cut all the way to the center of the trunk.** Complete the notch by making a straight cut about 6" below the first cut. Remove the triangle-shaped wedge.

TIP: PREVENTING KICKBACK

Kickback, a sudden movement in which a chain saw unexpectedly jumps up and back, is a leading cause of chain saw injuries. Kickback occurs when the nose of the guide bar makes contact with the object being cut. To prevent kickback, outfit your saw with a low-kick safety chain, avoid making contact with the nose of the bar and use both hands to grip the handles.

2. On the opposite side of the trunk, make the felling cut. Using the chain saw, make a straight cut about 2" above the base of the notch, leaving a 3" hinge at the center. **Do not saw completely through the trunk.**

Step C: Insert the Wedge & Drop the Tree
Immediately after making the felling cut, insert a wedge in the cut. (The wedge prevents the tree from becoming unstable.) Secure the wedge by tapping it into place with a maul. Make sure that the area surrounding the tree is clear. Push the tree toward the felling path, and run along the retreat path.

Step D: Remove the Remaining Branches
Standing on the opposite side of the trunk from the branch, adopt an open, balanced stance. Hold the chain saw close to you and saw down until the branch separates from the tree.

Step E: Cut the Trunk into Sections
Stand to one side of the trunk and cut down ⅔ of the way through the trunk. Roll the trunk onto its side. Finish the cut from the top, cutting down until the section breaks away.

C. *Insert a wedge into the cut. Push on the tree to start its fall, then move out of the way.*

D. *Remove each branch by cutting from the top, using a chain saw or bow saw.*

E. *To cut the trunk into sections, saw ⅔ of the way into the trunk. Roll the trunk over, then complete the cut from the top.*

Shaping

Grading

Unless your yard has the proper grade, or slope, rainwater can flow toward the foundation of your house—and possibly into your basement. An improper grade can also cause water to collect in low-lying areas, creating boggy spots where you'll have trouble growing grass and other plants. When graded correctly, your yard should have a gradual slope away from the house of about ¾" per horizontal foot.

Although the initial grading of a yard is usually done by a landscape contractor, you can do the work yourself to save money. The job is a bit time-consuming, but it isn't difficult. Typically, creating a grade at this stage involves spreading a 4" to 6" layer of topsoil over the yard, then distributing and smoothing it to slope away from the house.

Established landscapes often require regrading, especially if the house has settled. If you find signs of basement moisture problems or puddle-prone areas in the yard, you need to correct the slope. The measuring and grading techniques featured here will help you remove and distribute soil as needed.

TOOLS & MATERIALS

- Basic tools (page 16)
- Line level
- Grading rake
- Stakes
- String
- Tape
- Topsoil

HOW TO MEASURE & ESTABLISH A GRADE

Step A: Measure the Slope

1. Drive a pair of stakes into the soil, one at the base of the foundation, and another at least 8 ft. out into the yard along a straight line from the first stake.
2. Attach a string fitted with a line level to the stakes and adjust the string until it's level. Measure and flag the string with tape at 1-ft. intervals.

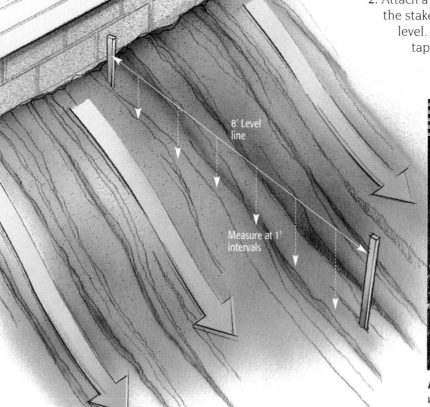

8' Level line

Measure at 1' intervals

A. To check the slope, level the string with a line level, then measure down at 1-ft. intervals.

3. Measure down from the string at the tape flags, recording your measurements as you work. Use these measurements as guidelines for adding or removing soil to create a correct grade.

Step B: Add & Distribute Soil

1. Starting at the base of the house, add soil to low areas until they reach the desired height.

2. Using a garden rake, evenly distribute the soil over a small area. Measure down from the 1-ft. markings as you work to make sure that you are creating a ¾" per 1-ft. pitch as you work.

3. Add and remove soil as needed, working away from the house until soil is evenly sloped. After you've completed an area, repeat steps A and B to grade the next section of your yard.

Step C: Lightly Tamp the Soil

Use a hand tamp to lightly compact the soil. Don't overtamp the soil or it could become too dense to grow a healthy lawn or plants.

Step D: Remove Debris

After all the soil is tamped, use a grading rake to remove any rocks or clumps. Starting at the foundation, pull the rake in a straight line down the slope. Dispose of any rocks or construction debris. Repeat the process, working on one section at a time until the entire area around the house is graded.

VARIATION: CREATING LEVEL AREAS

You may want to create some perfectly level areas for playing lawn sports such as croquet, badminton, volleyball and lawn bowling. Level areas also make safe play surfaces for small children and a good base for play structures.

Outline the perimeter of the area with evenly placed stakes. Extend a string fitted with a line level between a pair of stakes and adjust the string until it's level. At 2-ft. intervals, measure down from the marked areas of the string to the ground. Add and remove topsoil as necessary, distributing it with a garden rake until the surface under the string is level. Repeat the process until the entire area is leveled.

B. Beginning at the foundation, use a garden rake to distribute soil, checking and adjusting the slope as you work.

C. Use a hand tamp to lightly compact the soil in the graded area.

D. Pull a grading rake in a straight line down the slope to remove rocks, clumps and debris.

Shaping

Garden Steps

If you have a steep slope in a high-traffic area of your yard, adding garden steps makes the slope safer and more manageable. Or, if your yard has a long, continuous hill, you can add several sets of steps to get the same results. In addition to making your landscape more accessible, garden steps make your yard more attractive by creating visual interest.

Garden steps are built into an excavated portion of a slope or hill, flush with the surrounding ground. You can build steps from almost any hardscape mate-

rial: stone, brick, concrete, wood or even interlocking block. Our version uses two materials: wood and concrete. The design is simple—the steps are formed by a series of wood frames made from 5 × 6 landscape timbers. The frames are stacked on top of one another, following the run of the slope. After the frames are set in place, they're filled with concrete and given a finished texture.

The exact dimensions of the frames you build will depend on the height of your slope, the size of the timbers you're using and how wide and deep the steps need to be. Gradual slopes are best suited to a small number of broad steps. Steeper slopes require a larger number of narrower steps. To keep the stairs easy to use, the risers should be no more than 6" high, and the depth of the frame, also called the *tread depth*, should be at least 11".

PLANNING YOUR STEPS

Drive a tall stake into the ground at the bottom of the slope and adjust it until it's plumb. Then drive a shorter stake at the top of the slope. Position a straight 2 × 4 against the stakes, with one end touching the ground next to the top stake. Adjust the 2 × 4 so it's level, then attach it to the stakes with screws (see diagram, left). Measure from the ground to the bottom of the 2 × 4 to find the total vertical rise of the stairway. Divide the total rise by the actual thickness of the timbers to find the

TOOLS & MATERIALS

- Basic tools (page 16)
- Hand tamp
- Reciprocating saw
- Staple gun
- Wood/ concrete float
- Masonry trowel
- Masonry edging tool
- Stiff-bristled brush
- Stakes and string
- 5 × 6 landscape timbers
- 12" spikes
- ¾" galvanized pipe
- Plastic sheeting
- Compactible gravel
- Concrete mix

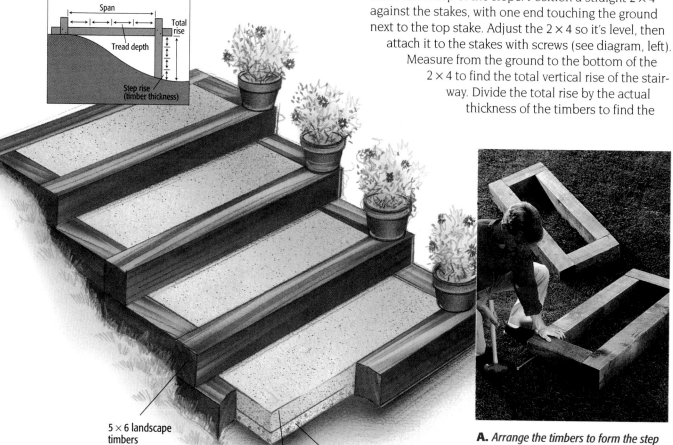

5 × 6 landscape timbers

Compactible gravel

Concrete

A. *Arrange the timbers to form the step frame and end nail them together, using 12" spikes.*

number of steps required. Round off fractions to the nearest full number.

Measure along the 2 × 4, between the stakes, to find the total horizontal span. Divide the span by the number of steps to find the tread depth. If the tread depth comes out to less than 11", revise the step layout to extend it.

HOW TO BUILD GARDEN STEPS

Step A: Build the Frames

Use a reciprocating saw to cut timbers, then assemble the step frames with 12" spikes. In our design, the front timber runs the full width of the step; while the back timber is 10" shorter than the front and fits between the side timbers.

Step B: Outline the Step Run

1. Mark the sides of the site with stakes and string. Position the stakes at the front edge of the bottom step and the back edge of the top step.
2. Outline the excavation for the first step at the base of the slope, using stakes and string. Remember that the excavation will be larger than the overall tread depth, since the back timber in the frame will be covered by the front timber of the next step.

Step C: Excavate & Install the First Frame

1. Excavate the area for the first frame, creating a flat bed with a very slight forward slope, dropping about ⅛" from back to front. The front of the excavation should be no more than 2" deep. Tamp the soil down

TIP: PLANNING YOUR GARDEN STEPS

To simplify the building process, take all necessary measurements, then make a sketch of the site. Indicate the rise, tread depth and width of each step. Remember that actual timber dimensions may vary from the nominal measurements.

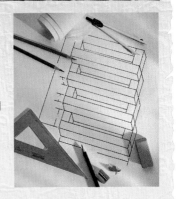

firmly, using a hand tamp.
2. Set the timber frame into the excavation. Use a level to make sure that the front and back timbers are level, and that the frame slopes slightly forward.
3. Using a spade bit, drill two 1" guide holes in the front timber and the back timber, 1 ft. from the ends. Anchor the steps to the ground by driving a 2½-ft. length of ¾" pipe through each guide hole until the pipe is flush with the timber.

Step D: Add the Second Frame

1. Excavate for the next step, making sure the bottom of the excavation is even with the top edge of the frame you installed for the first step.

B. *Outline the area for the steps with stakes and string, then measure the height of the slope.*

C. *Excavate the area for the first step, and install the first step frame.*

D. *Excavate the area for the next step, and assemble the frame. Stake the second frame to the first with 12" spikes.*

Garden Steps (cont.)

VARIATION: BRICK-FILLED STEPS

If pavers are used elsewhere in your landscape, you may prefer to repeat that element by filling your wood step frames with sand-set pavers. Other variations you can try are shown on the opposite page.

2. Position the second step frame in the excavation, lining up the front of the frame directly over the rear timber of the first frame.

3. Nail the first frame to the second with three 12" spikes. Drill guide holes and drive two pipes through the back timber to anchor the second frame in place.

Step E: Place the Remaining Frames

1. Excavate and install the remaining steps in the run. The back of the last step should be flush with the ground at the top of the slope.

2. Staple plastic over the timbers to protect them while the concrete is being poured. Cut away the plastic from the frame openings.

3. Pour a 2" layer of compactible gravel into each frame, and use a scrap 2 × 4 to smooth it out.

Step F: Fill the Steps with Concrete

1. Mix concrete and shovel it into the bottom frame, flush with the top of the timbers. Work the concrete lightly with a garden rake to help remove air bubbles, but don't overwork it.

2. Screed the concrete smooth by dragging a 2 × 4 across the top of the frame. If necessary, add concrete to the low areas and screed the surface again until it is smooth and free of low spots.

3. Use an edging tool to smooth the cracks between the concrete and the timbers.

4. Pour concrete into remaining steps, screeding and edging each step before moving on to the next.

Step G: Finish the Surface & Cure the Concrete

1. While the concrete is still wet, create a textured, nonskid surface by drawing a clean, stiff-bristled broom across its surface. Brush each surface only one time, and avoid overlapping brush marks.

2. Remove the plastic from around the timbers.

3. When the concrete has hardened, mist it with water, cover it with plastic, and let it cure for one week.

4. After the concrete has cured, remove the plastic.

E. *Cover the completed framework with plastic. Pour and smooth a 2" layer of compactible gravel in each frame.*

F. *Shovel concrete into the first frame, then work it with a garden rake to remove air bubbles.*

G. *Texture the surface of the concrete by drawing a stiff-bristled broom across it in one sweeping motion.*

VARIATION: GARDEN STEPS

These wood-and-paver steps complement the colorful border that surrounds them.

These stone steps suit the rustic site perfectly.

These curving wood steps echo the informal tone of the rest of the landscape.

The formality of these brick steps contrasts nicely with the riot of flowers.

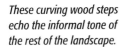

These attractive steps illustrate how effectively materials such as cement and stone can be combined.

Shaping

Retaining Wall

Retaining walls are often used to manage steep slopes in a landscape. They not only prevent erosion, but also create flat space for a garden bed, patio or a hedge. Retaining walls are not limited to sloped yards, however. They can also be used to add the illusion of slope to a flat yard. After these decorative retaining walls are constructed, the area behind the wall is backfilled with soil for a planting area.

Interlocking block is the easiest material to work with when constructing retaining walls. The biggest advantage of interlocking block is that it doesn't require mortar. Blocks are available in many styles and colors that will blend with or provide an accent to your landscape. Some of these products have a natural rock finish that resembles the texture of cut stone, which adds a distinctive touch to a wall.

Although the wall itself does not require any type of fixative, the coordinating capstones are held securely in place by construction-grade adhesive. We've used coordinating capstones for this project, but you could also use mortared natural stone, which creates a pleasing contrast.

Limit the height of retaining walls to 4 ft. Taller walls are subject to thousands of pounds of pressure from the weight of the soil and water. They require special building techniques and permits, and are best constructed by professionals. If your slope is greater than 4 ft., build a series of terraced walls over the course of the slope, instead of a single, tall wall.

HOW TO BUILD A RETAINING WALL

Step A: Excavate the Site

1. Excavate the slope to create a level area for the retaining wall. Allow at least 12" of space for the gravel backfill between the back of the wall and the hillside.
2. Use stakes to mark the front edge of the wall at the ends, and at any corners or curves. Connect the stakes with string, and use a line level to check the string, adjusting until it's level.

TOOLS & MATERIALS

- Basic tools (page 16)
- Rented plate compactor
- Stakes
- String
- Line level
- Landscape fabric
- Compactible gravel
- Interlocking block
- Perforated drain tile
- Gravel
- Hand tamp
- Construction-grade adhesive
- Capstones
- Caulk gun

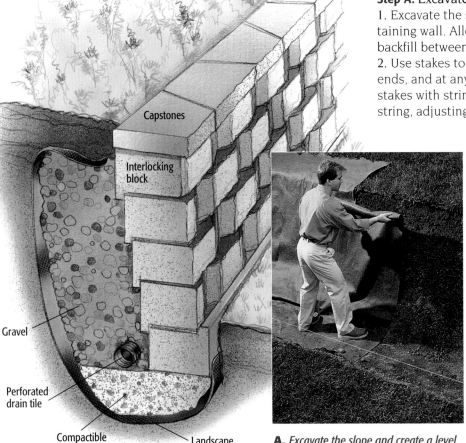

Capstones

Interlocking block

Gravel

Perforated drain tile

Compactible gravel

Landscape fabric

A. *Excavate the slope and create a level trench at the base. Line the excavation with strips of landscape fabric.*

B. *Lay the first row of interlocking block over the compacted gravel base in the trench, checking with a level as you work.*

30

3. Dig a trench for the first row of block. Make the trench 8" deeper than the thickness of the block. Measure down from the string as you work to make sure the trench remains level.

4. Line the excavated area with strips of landscape fabric cut 3 ft. longer that the planned height of the wall. Overlap the strips by at least 6".

Step B: Build a Base & Lay the First Row

1. Spread a 6" layer of compactible gravel into the trench. Compact the gravel, using a plate compactor.

2. Lay the first row of blocks into the trench, aligning the front edges with the string. If you're using flanged blocks, install the first row of blocks upside down and backward in the trench.

3. Check the blocks frequently with a level, and adjust them by adding or removing gravel.

Step C: Install Drain Tile & Add Rows

1. Lay the second row of blocks according to the manufacturer's instructions, making sure the joints are staggered with the course below. As you work, check to make sure the blocks are level.

2. Add 1" to 2" of gravel, as needed, to create a slight downward pitch as the drain tile runs toward the outlet.

3. Place perforated drain tile on top of the gravel, about 6" behind the blocks, with the perforations facing down. Make sure that at least one end of the pipe is unobstructed so runoff water can escape.

4. Lay the additional rows until the wall is about 18" high, offsetting vertical joints in successive rows.

TIP: CREATING HALF-BLOCKS

Half-blocks are often needed for making corners, and to ensure that vertical joints between blocks are staggered between rows. To make a half-block, score a full block with a circular saw outfitted with a masonry blade, then break the blocks along the scored line with a maul and chisel.

5. Fill behind the wall with coarse gravel, and pack it down with the hand tamp.

Step D: Lay the Remaining Rows & Backfill

1. Lay the remaining rows of block, except the cap row, backfilling with gravel and packing it down with a hand tamp as you work.

2. Fold the landscape fabric down over the gravel backfill. Add a thin layer of topsoil over the landscape fabric, then lightly pack down the soil, using the hand tamp.

3. Fold any excess landscape fabric back over the tamped soil.

Step E: Add the Capstones

1. Apply construction adhesive to the top blocks. Lay the capstones in place.

2. Use topsoil to fill in behind the wall and to fill in the trench at the base of the wall.

3. Add sod or other plants, as desired, above and below the wall.

C. *Lay a section of perforated drain tile behind the wall over the gravel, then lay the remaining rows of blocks.*

D. *Fold the excess landscape fabric over the gravel, then cover it with a layer of soil. Compress the soil with a hand tamp.*

E. *Apply adhesive along the top blocks, then lay the capstones so the joints are staggered with those below.*

Shaping

Berm

Without imaginative treatment, flat yards can be short on privacy as well as style or character. Creating a *berm*, a built-up planting area with sloped sides, resolves several issues common to flat yards. A berm screens out undesirable views, adds interesting contours and even absorbs some of the noise from passing traffic.

Berms can be functional, but they can also serve strictly as ornamental features. An ornamental berm acts as a focal point, adding interest and color to your lawn. In colder climates, a berm planted expressly for winter beauty is an especially welcomed addition to a snow-covered landscape. In warmer climates, they can be planted with specimen trees that change with the seasons. Berms for desert climates often showcase a variety of ground cover and cacti.

Whether you're creating a functional or an ornamental berm, keep in mind that the most attractive examples have gentle slopes and irregular shapes that accent the surrounding yard. If possible, avoid creating a steep or angular berm—these tend to look awkward, and may even erode over time. If you're planning to construct a particularly high or wide berm, carefully position it so that water drains efficiently. Avoid building a berm around an existing tree. Arborists caution that covering a tree's roots with more than 4" of topsoil can "smother" and eventually kill a tree.

Since building a berm involves creating an elevated area, you'll undoubtedly need to add soil. Before using soil from another area of the yard, collect samples and have a soil test conducted to make sure the soil is capable of supporting trees and plants. You may be better off purchasing high-grade topsoil from a soil contractor and having it delivered.

TOOLS & MATERIALS

- Basic tools (page 16)
- Flexible plastic edging
- Stakes
- Hand tamp
- Plantings
- Mulch

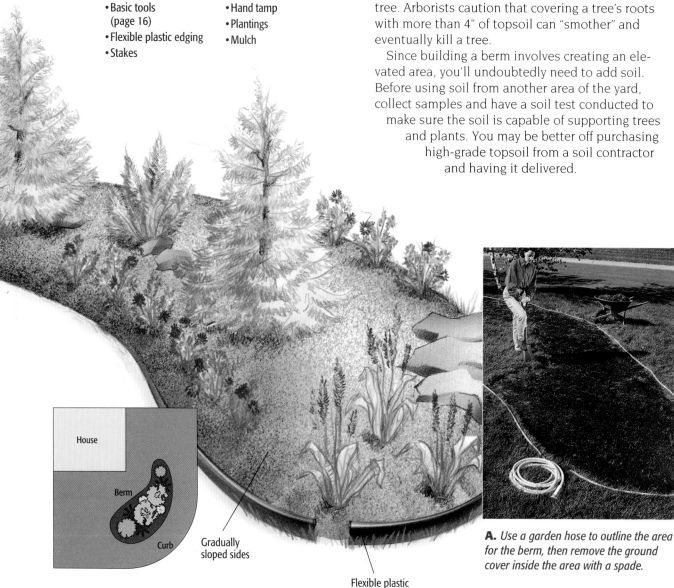

House

Berm

Curb

Gradually sloped sides

Flexible plastic edging

A. *Use a garden hose to outline the area for the berm, then remove the ground cover inside the area with a spade.*

HOW TO CREATE A BERM

Step A: Prepare the Site

Using a hose or rope, create an outline for the planned berm. Using a spade, remove all grass or ground cover growing inside the outline. If the berm is large, you may want to use a sod cutter.

Step B: Install Plastic Edging

With a trenching spade, dig a trench around the perimeter of the berm area, just wide enough to install the flexible plastic edging. To hold the edging in place, use a maul to drive stakes through the bottom rim of the edging.

Step C: Add the Soil & Shape the Berm

1. Fill the outlined area with topsoil. Using a garden rake, distribute the soil so that the berm is 18" to 24" tall at the highest point. When all the necessary soil is added, grade the sides into a gradual slope.

2. Using a hand tamp, compact the entire surface of the berm, then water the soil to further compress it.

Step D: Install Plants & Add Mulch

1. Plant trees, shrubs or other plants in the berm, using the planting techniques shown in "Trees" (page 66), "Hedges" (page 64) and "Garden Beds" (page 100).

2. Apply a 2" to 3" layer of mulch over the surface of the berm to prevent weeds and retain moisture.

VARIATION: EDGING MATERIALS

A variety of edging materials is available. Look for ways to repeat existing materials in your landscape. Here are a few commonly used options:

A. Cut timbers can be used as edging on straight garden beds.

B. Flagstones are relatively inexpensive. Their rough texture works well in informal, country or cottage-style landscapes.

C. Geometric pavers make an attractive, durable edging.

D. Bricks are a traditional material used in formal-looking landscapes. They can be arranged end to end, side by side, or even upright for a slightly raised edging.

E. Concrete rubble scavenged from demolition sites can be laid broken side up to make an inexpensive, textured edging.

F. Cut stones (called ashlars) are a premium building material that lends a unique, tailored look to berms.

G. Plastic landscape edging can be purchased at landscape and gardening centers.

B. *Place the edging in the trench along the perimeter of the berm, then drive edging stakes through the bottom lip.*

C. *Fill the area with soil, then grade it into a gradual slope with a garden rake. Use a hand tamp to compress the soil.*

D. *Arrange the plantings on the surface, then plant them in the berm. Apply 2" to 3" layer of mulch over the entire surface.*

Shaping
Drainage Swale

If your yard has areas where rainwater collects and creates boggy spots or has slopes that send runoff water into unwanted places, you need to improve or re-direct its drainage. You can fill small low-lying areas by top-dressing them with black soil, but in large areas, the best solution is to create a swale.

A swale is a shallow ditch that carries water away from the yard to a designated collection area, usually a gutter, sewer catch bin, stream or lake. Some communities have restrictions regarding redirecting

runoff water, so contact your city or county inspector's office to discuss your plans before you begin. This is especially important if you're planning a swale that empties into a natural water source, such as a stream, pond or lake.

If you're building a swale between your house and a neighboring yard, talk to your neighbor about the project before you begin. If drainage is a problem in their yard as well, they may be willing to share the expense and the work of the project.

Building a swale is relatively simple, but it involves the labor of digging a trench. We'll show you how to construct the swale using a shovel, but there are rental tools that you might want to use instead. For larger yards or those with very dense soil, renting a trencher is an option worth considering. This machine, which can be adjusted to dig to an approximate depth, makes quick work of loosening the soil. If you decide to use a trencher, you'll still need to use a shovel to create the "V" shape and to smooth the sides of the trench, as pictured below.

Another machine you may want to rent is a sod cutter, which cuts the sod into even strips that can be replaced when the swale is complete. If you plan to

TOOLS & MATERIALS

- Basic tools (page 16)
- Stakes
- Trenching spade
- Sod cutter (optional)

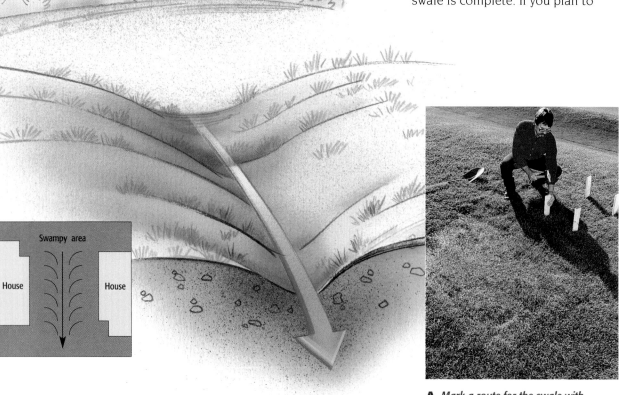

A. *Mark a route for the swale with stakes, making sure that the outlet for the water is at the lowest point.*

reuse the sod, store it in a shady area and keep it slightly moist until you replant it.

HOW TO MAKE A DRAINAGE SWALE

Step A: Mark the Route

After identifying the problem area, use stakes to mark a swale route that directs water toward an appropriate runoff area. To promote drainage, the outlet of the swale must be lower than any point in the problem area or along the planned route.

Step B: Remove the Sod

Carefully remove the sod from the outlined area. Set it aside and keep it moist, so that it can be replaced when the swale is complete.

Step C: Dig the Trench

Following the marked route, dig a 6"-deep "V"-shaped trench with wide, rounded sides. Shape the trench so it slopes gradually downward toward the outlet, making sure that the bottom and sides of the trench are smooth. Set the topsoil aside for other projects.

Step D: Replace the Sod

Lay the sod back into the trench. Compress it thoroughly, so the roots make contact with the soil and there are no air pockets beneath it. Water the sod and keep it moist for several weeks.

VARIATION: SWALE WITH DRAIN TILE

If you have very dense soil with a high clay content or severe drainage problems, you'll need to lay perforated drain pipe in the trench for the swale. Follow these steps to make a swale with drain tile:

Step A:

Dig a 1-ft.-deep trench, angled downward to the outlet point. Line the trench with landscape fabric. Spread a 2" layer of coarse gravel along the bottom of the swale, then lay perforated drain pipe over the gravel, with the perforations facing down. Cover the pipe with a 5" layer of gravel, then wrap landscape fabric over the top of the gravel.

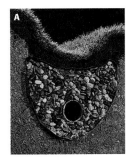

Step B:

Cover the swale with soil and the original or fresh sod. Set a splash block at the outlet under the exposed end of the drain pipe to distribute the runoff water and prevent erosion.

B. *Carefully remove the sod with a spade and set it aside, keeping it moist until you're ready to replace it.*

C. *Dig a 6"-deep trench that slopes to the center, creating a "V" shape. Use the shovel to smooth the sides as you work.*

D. *Replace the sod, compressing it against the soil. Water the sod and keep it moist for several weeks.*

Shaping

Dry Well

A dry well is a simple but clever method for channeling excess water out of low-lying or water-laden areas, such as the ground beneath a gutter downspout. A dry well system typically consists of a buried drain tile running from a catch basin positioned at the problem spot to a collection container some distance away.

A dry well system is easy to install and surprisingly inexpensive. In the project shown here, a perforated plastic drain tile carries water from a catch basin to a dry well fashioned from a plastic trash can, which has been punctured, then filled with stone rubble. The runoff water percolates into the soil as it makes its way along the drain pipe and through the dry well.

HOW TO INSTALL A DRY WELL
Step A: Dig the Trench

1. Using stakes, mark a path running from the problem area to the location of the dry well. Carefully remove a 12" strip of sod and set it aside, keeping it moist so you can reuse it later. Dig a trench, 10" wide and 14" deep, along the staked path.

TOOLS & MATERIALS

- Basic tools (page 16)
- Line level
- Jig saw
- Stakes

- String
- Landscape fabric
- Gravel
- Plastic trash can

- Large stones
- Catch basin
- Perforated drain tile

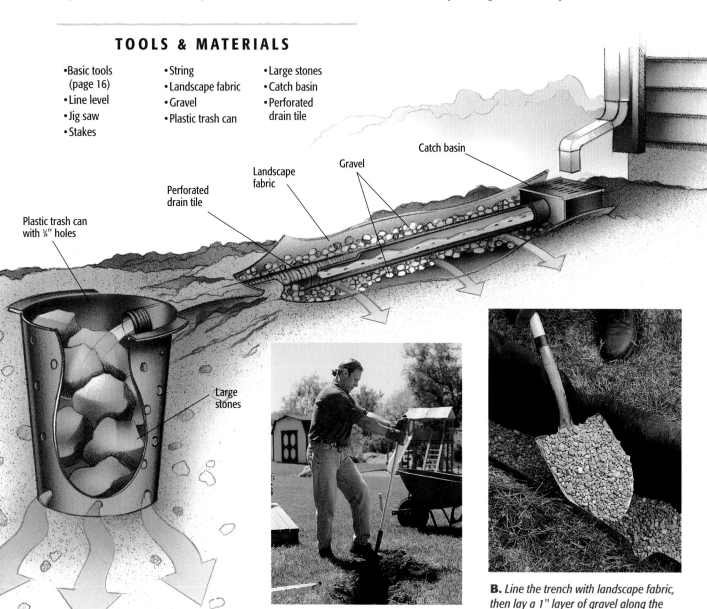

Catch basin

Gravel

Landscape fabric

Perforated drain tile

Plastic trash can with ¾" holes

Large stones

A. Dig a 10"-wide, 14"-deep trench along the planned route from the catch basin to the dry well.

B. Line the trench with landscape fabric, then lay a 1" layer of gravel along the bottom of the trench.

2. Slope the trench slightly toward the dry well, about 2" for every 8 ft., to ensure that water flows easily along the drain tile. To check the slope, place a stake at each end of the trench, then tie a string between the stakes. Use a line level to level the string, then measure down from it at 2-ft. intervals. Add or remove soil as needed to adjust the slope of the trench.

3. Remove the sod in a circle, 4" wider than the dry well container, then dig a hole at least 4" deeper than the container's height.

Step B: Lay the Drain Tile

1. Line the trench and hole with landscape fabric, folding the excess fabric back over each side of the trench and around the edges of the hole.

2. Lay a 1" layer of gravel along the bottom of the trench, then lay the drain tile in place, with the perforations facing down.

Step C: Create the Dry Well

1. About 3" from the top, trace the outline of the drain tile onto the side of the trash can, then use a jig saw to cut a hole. Using a power drill and a ¾" bit, drill drainage holes through the sides and bottom of the trash can, one hole every 4" to 6".

2. Place the trash can in the hole, positioning it so the large hole faces the trench. Insert the drain tile, perforated side down, with at least 2" of the tile

T I P :

Gravel comes in two forms: rough and smooth. When buying gravel for shaping projects, select rough gravel. Smooth gravel typically is used as a decorative ground cover. When used for shaping projects, it tends to slide toward the middle of the trench. Rough gravel clings to the sides of the trench, creating a more even drainage layer.

extending inside the trash can.

3. Fill the trash can with large stones. Arrange the top layer of stones so they are flat in the container.

4. Fold the landscape fabric over the rocks, then fill the hole with soil.

Step D: Connect the Catch Basin

At the other end of the trench, opposite the dry well, connect the catch basin to the drain tile. Position the catch basin so excess water will flow directly into it.

Step E: Refill the Trench

1. Fill the trench with gravel until the drain tile is covered by 1" of gravel. Fold the edges of the landscape cloth down over the gravel-covered drain tile.

2. Fill the trench with the soil you removed earlier.

3. Replace the sod, lightly tamp it with the back of a shovel, then water it thoroughly.

C. *Prepare the dry well container, then place it in the excavation, insert the drain tile and fill it with large rocks.*

D. *Attach a catch basin to the drain tile opening, and position the basin to collect the excess water in the problem area.*

E. *Cover the drain tile with 1" of gravel, then backfill the trench with soil and fold the landscape fabric over it.*

Utilities

Inside our homes, utilities make our lives easier and more comfortable. Similarly, plumbing and electricity can make outdoor rooms more functional and enjoyable. The idea of extending electricity and plumbing outdoors may seem daunting at first, but it's surprisingly simple.

Working with your existing electrical wiring, you can easily add a floodlight onto your house or garage and install an attractive low-voltage lighting system. Armed with a few basic wiring and plumbing techniques, you can go a step further and install new standard electrical or plumbing lines virtually anywhere in your yard.

With these new utility lines, you can create an outlet for powering electric appliances and tools, install a garden spigot for washing tools and even add an in-ground sprinkler system to simplify watering chores. Although adding a sprinkler system may sound difficult, there are a number of affordable do-it-yourself products available. If you install a system with an electric timer, you can program your sprinkler system to water your yard at any time of day, for any amount of time you wish.

In addition to being convenient, utilities also make your yard safer. Carefully placed GFCI receptacles eliminate the need to stretch extension cords across the lawn and protect against power surges and accidental shock. Garden spigots bring water within easy reach of planting beds and cleanup areas. Floodlights and landscape lighting increase security and help people navigate pathways and stairs at night.

The demonstrations in this chapter show you basic techniques for tapping into your home's plumbing and electrical systems and extending water and voltage lines into any area of your yard. If you aren't familiar with basic plumbing and wiring techniques, you may want to consult how-to books on these subjects, many of which are available at home centers, book stores and libraries.

One word of caution: always have underground utility lines marked before you begin projects that involve digging.

IN THIS CHAPTER:

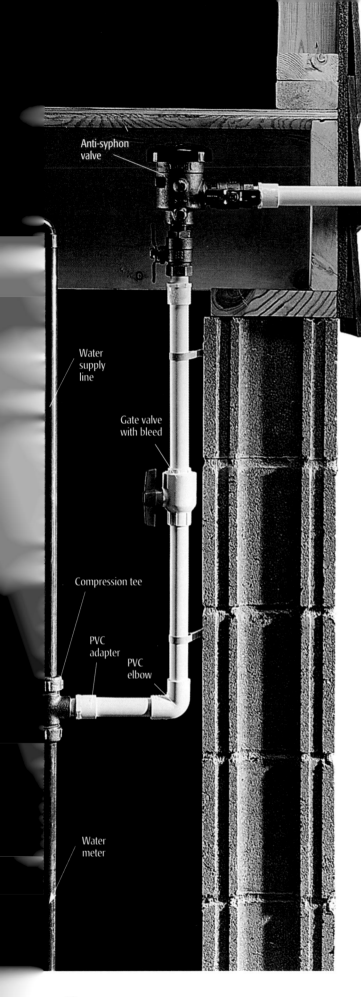

Anti-syphon
valve

Water
supply
line

Gate valve
with bleed

Compression tee

PVC
adapter

PVC
elbow

Water
meter

Sprinkler System Basics

The most efficient way to water your yard is with an underground sprinkler system. Unlike hand watering or the hose-and-sprinkler method, sprinkler systems distribute water evenly and accurately, conserving water in the process.

Home supply centers and irrigation system catalogs sell affordable, high-quality kits and sprinkler system parts designed for do-it-yourself installation. Most of the DIY sprinkler systems now available have similar components and operate in much the same way. The following information will help you design and plan a customized sprinkler system for your yard.

A basic sprinkler system is connected to your home's water line by a *connecting line* that distributes water to a grouping of sprinkler control valves, called a *valve manifold*. The control valves are operated either manually or by a timer; each control valve supplies water to a grouping of *sprinkler heads*, called a circuit. The sprinkler heads are attached to the sprinkler line by flexible piping.

DETERMINING GPM

The first thing you'll need to do is determine your water system's GPM (gallons per minute) measurement. Your water system's GPM will determine the size pipe you'll need and the number of sprinkler heads that can be assigned to a single circuit.

To assess your water system's GPM, measure how long it takes to fill a one-gallon bucket from your outside faucet. Make sure there is no water running elsewhere, inside or outside the house, then turn the faucet on full force. To calculate the GPM, divide 60

seconds by the amount of time it takes to fill the bucket. For example, if it takes 6 seconds to fill the one-gallon bucket, the GPM is 60/6 seconds, or 10 GPM.

GALLONS-PER-MINUTE (GPM) TABLE

GPM Flow	Control Valve Size	PVC Pipe Size	Flexible PE Pipe Size
0-8	3/4"	3/4"	3/4"
9-12	3/4"	3/4"	1"
13-16	1"	1"	1 1/4"
17-28	1"	1 1/4"	1 1/2"

This cutaway photo illustrates a typical construction for a connecting line installed between the water supply line and the sprinkler system valve manifold.

SELECTING PIPES & CONTROL VALVES

Use the table on page 40 to determine what size valves and piping you'll need to buy, based on your GPM measurement. Select either semirigid PVC or schedule 40 pipe for the connecting line. You can choose either flexible polyethylene (PE) or PVC pipe for the sprinkler circuit piping—which includes the sprinkler line and the pipes to the sprinkler heads.

There are several other factors you'll need to consider when selecting the control valves. Automatic systems use a different style of control valve than manual systems. And Plumbing Code restrictions in your area may require that you use anti-syphon valves that prevent water backflow.

CHOOSING SPRINKLER HEADS

Manufacturers offer a variety of sprinkler heads, each with a different broadcast range and watering pattern. Some styles mount above the ground while others pop up from below the ground.

Each sprinkler head has a GPM measurement. For each circuit, select sprinkler heads with GPM ratings that add up to a total of no more that 75% of your water system's total GPM rating. This will ensure that no damage will occur to either the sprinkler system or your home's water system. So, for example, if your home's GPM measurement is 10, choose sprinkler heads so the total GPM assigned to the circuit does not exceed 7.5.

ASSIGNING THE SPRINKLER HEADS

Draw a map of your yard, and divide the areas that will need watering into squares or rectangles. Begin drawing the locations of the sprinkler heads that will water these areas. To ensure even coverage, position the sprinklers so that their range of coverage overlaps slightly.

MAPPING THE SPRINKLER CIRCUITS

Designate a spot for the control valve manifold, preferably close to an accessible plumbing line. Map the route from your home's water supply line to the control valve manifold.

Group the the sprinkler heads into circuits and draw the piping for each circuit. Draw a line extending from the control valve manifold to each circuit. Add lines branching out from the piping to each sprinkler head in the circuit (diagram, above right). Make sure the total GPM for all sprinkler heads in each circuit doesn't exceed 75% of your water system's GPM.

Sprinkler system components, such as these from Rain Bird™, are sold at home improvement centers and by mail order.

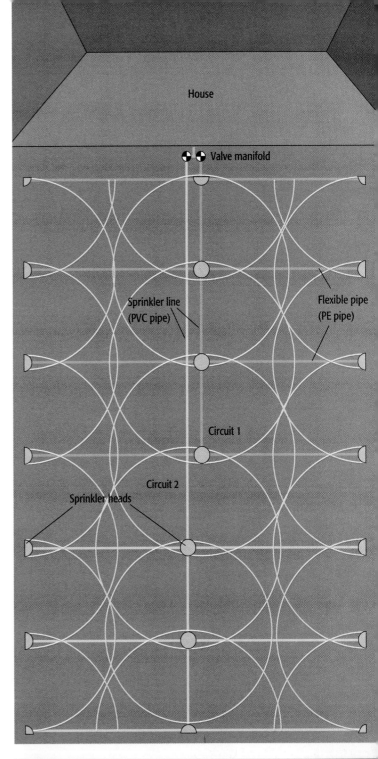

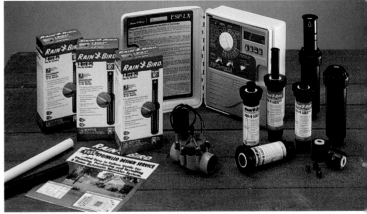

Sprinkler System

HOW TO INSTALL A SPRINKLER SYSTEM
Step A: Connect to the Water Supply System
1. Dig a 10"-deep hole for the valve manifold box, as indicated on the map you developed (page 41).
2. Drill a 1"-diameter hole through the wall where you'll be running the pipe from the water supply system to the valve manifold.
3. Turn off the water supply at the water meter, then cut into a cold water supply pipe and install a compression tee fitting.
4. Measure and cut the components to run a cold water line from the tee fitting through the hole you cut in the wall. The exact components will vary, depending on the configuration of your plumbing system, but you'll need several lengths of PVC pipe, PVC elbows, a PVC gate valve with a bleed fitting and a brass vacuum breaker. You'll also need three threaded PVC adapters for the points where plastic pipe is joined to metal.
5. Assemble the branch line by threading the PVC adapters onto the metal components, using solvent glue to join the PVC pipes to the adapters and to any elbows needed to extend the branch line through the hole leading outside the house. Once the branch line is in place, use pipe straps to anchor the new pipes to interior framing members or walls.
6. From outside, attach a PVC elbow and a length of PVC pipe to extend the supply line down the wall. Anchor the pipe to the wall, using pipe straps.
7. Connect a PVC elbow fitting and straight length of pipe to extend the water supply line horizontally into the center of the location for the valve manifold box.

Step B: Make the Manifold & Install the Valve Box
1. Use PVC elbows, tee fittings and pipes to split the water supply line into a manifold that includes one arm for each of the control valves.
2. Connect the sprinkler control valves, following manufacturer's instructions. Some valves use threaded fittings; others are solvent-glued.
3. Test the water line and connections

TOOLS & MATERIALS

- Basic tools, page 16
- Tubing cutter
- Copper compression tee
- Schedule 40 PVC pipe
- PVC elbows

- PVC gate valves with bleed (2)
- Brass vacuum breaker
- Threaded PVC adapters
- PVC solvent glue
- Pipe straps
- Valve boxes (2)

- PVC tee fitting and elbow
- Sprinkler control valves
- Stakes
- Spray paint
- Outdoor grade PE pipe
- Sprinkler heads

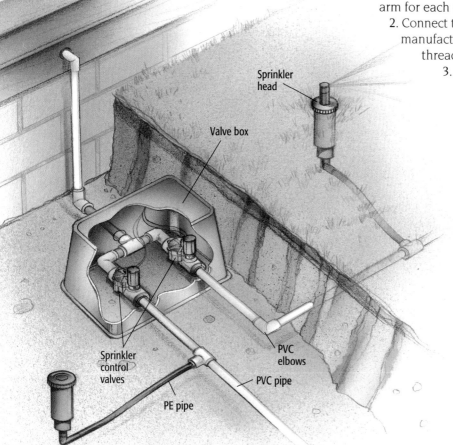

Sprinkler head

Valve box

Sprinkler control valves

PE pipe

PVC pipe

PVC elbows

A. *Tie into the water supply line with a compression tee, then assemble the connecting line that leads to the valves.*

for leaks by closing the control valves, then opening the gate valve and the main water supply valve inside your house. If you discover leaks, turn off the water, drain the system, and make any necessary repairs.

4. Place the valve box over the control valve manifold, pushing it firmly into the ground.

5. If you're installing an automatic system, mount the timer to a wall inside the house or garage, close to a 120-volt receptacle. Run a wire from the timer out to the control valves. Following manufacturer's instructions, connect each of the control valves to the timer.

6. Place the cover back on top of the valve box.

Step C: Lay Out the Circuits

1. Using your map as a reference, mark the locations of the sprinkler heads with stakes.

2. Mark the path for the circuit piping leading from the control valves into the yard, and for the piping leading from the circuit lines to the sprinkler heads.

3. Dig a hole for the second valve box, which will provide system drainage. Locate this box at the lowest point within the system.

4. Dig trenches for the circuit piping, making each trench 8" to 12" deep. The trenches should slope ⅛" per foot toward the house.

TIP:

If an area assigned to a single sprinkler head includes a tree, bush or other obstruction, add sprinkler heads to provide coverage behind it.

5. Dig trenches, 8" to 12" deep, extending between the sprinkler heads and the circuit piping. The trenches should slope ⅛" per foot as they run toward the circuit piping.

Step D: Install the Circuit Piping & Sprinkler Heads

1. Measure and cut the PVC piping for each circuit. Attach the pipe to the control valves and lay it in the trenches. At the trench with the second valve box, install a gate valve with a bleed on the end of the pipe.

2. Measure, cut and lay the flexible PE pipe running from the circuit pipes to each of the sprinkler heads.

3. Attach the flexible PE pipe to the PVC pipe with PVC tee fittings. Using a threaded PVC adapter, attach the PE pipe to the sprinkler head.

4. Assemble all the sprinkler heads for the first circuit. If you're using pop-up sprinklers, temporarily tie them to small stakes.

5. Turn the water supply back on and open the gate valve. Turn on the circuit control valve and check for any leaks. Adjust the sprinkler heads as necessary to provide even coverage.

6. Install and test the remaining circuits. When all of the adjustments are made, complete the installation according to the manufacturer's directions.

7. Refill the trenches, replace the sod, and water it.

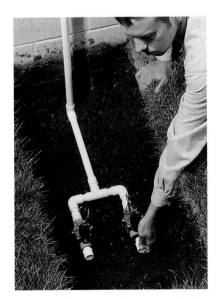

B. *Assemble the control valve manifold and attach it to the connecting line. Attach the control valves.*

C. *Mark the route for the circuit piping. At the lowest circuit, dig a pit for a valve box, then finish digging the trench.*

D. *Install PVC tee fittings with adapters to the circuit piping. Attach the flexible PE pipe to the adapters and the sprinklers.*

Garden Spigot

You may already have a hose spigot or two attached to the foundation of your house, but adding one or two spigots to various areas of your outdoor home brings water right to the areas where you typically water plants or clean up garden equipment.

Our version of a garden spigot can be located almost anywhere in your yard. To install it, you'll need to run a branch line off your home's water supply system, through the foundation or exterior wall, and along an underground trench to a hose spigot anchored to a post, which is embedded in a bucket of concrete at the end of the plumbing run.

The project illustrated here uses copper pipe for the above-ground parts of the run, and PE pipe for the buried sections. Your local Plumbing Code may have requirements for the types of pipe you can use, so check it before you begin. Also, if local Plumbing Code requires it, be sure to apply for required permits and arrange for necessary inspections.

TOOLS & MATERIALS

- Basic tools (page 16)
- Spade bit
- Tubing cutter
- Soldering materials
- Copper tee fittings
- ¾" copper pipe
- Brass gate valve with bleed
- Copper elbows
- Brass vacuum breaker

- Stakes
- Valve boxes (2)
- Gravel
- ¾" PE pipe
- Insert couplings
- Stainless steel clamps
- 4-ft. 4 × 4 post
- Spigot
- Pipe straps

- Concrete
- 2-gallon plastic bucket
- Barbed PVC tee fittings with threaded outlet and plug (2)
- Male-threaded copper adapters (2)
- Female-threaded PE adapters (2)

HOW TO INSTALL A GARDEN SPIGOT

Step A: Connect to the Water Supply System

1. Plan a convenient route from the water supply line to the location you've chosen for the spigot. Drill a 1" hole through the exterior wall, near where you'll be running the pipe from the water supply system to the valve box. Turn off the water at the main supply valve near the water meter.

2. Remove a small section of the cold water pipe and install a tee fitting. Install a straight length of copper pipe, then a gate valve with a bleed fitting.

3. Use straight lengths of pipe and elbow fittings to extend the branch line through the hole in the wall, installing a vacuum breaker at some convenient point along the way.

Step B: Lay Out the Branch Line & Install the Valve Box

1. Outside the house, stake a line marking the path

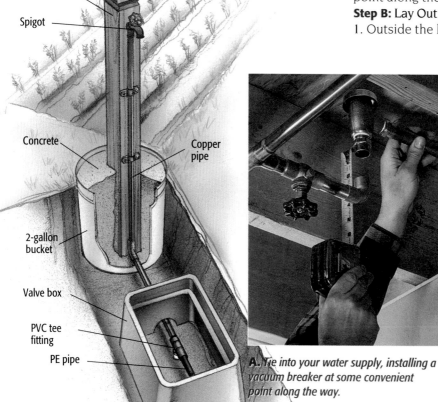

4 × 4 post

Spigot

Concrete

Copper pipe

2-gallon bucket

Valve box

PVC tee fitting

PE pipe

A. Tie into your water supply, installing a vacuum breaker at some convenient point along the way.

B. Extend the branch line through the wall and down into the trench. Install the valve box.

for the pipe run to the spigot location.

2. Use a trenching spade to remove sod for an 8"- to 12"-wide trench along the marked route. Dig a trench at least 10" deep and sloping toward the house at a rate of ⅛" per foot.

3. Dig a hole for a valve box, directly below the point where the branch line exits the house.

4. Measure, cut and attach copper pipe and elbows, extending the branch line down to the bottom of the trench and out 12".

5. Install a valve box with the top flush to the ground. Lay a 4" layer of gravel in the bottom of the valve box.

Step C: Run the Supply Line to the Spigot Location

1. Dig a hole at the spigot location, sized to hold a valve box and the bucket. Install the other valve box.

2. Lay ¾" PE pipe in the trench, running from the valve box by the house to the valve box at the spigot location. Use couplings and stainless steel clamps when necessary to join two lengths of pipe.

Step D: Install the Spigot

1. Cut a 3-ft. piece of copper pipe and secure it to one side of the 4 × 4 post, using pipe straps. Mount the spigot on the top of the pipe, then attach an elbow to the bottom of the pipe.

2. Using a drill and spade bit, drill a 1" hole in the side of a 2-gallon bucket, 1" above the bottom.

3. Position the post in the bucket, with the pipe facing toward the hole. Measure, cut and attach a length of pipe to the elbow at the bottom of the post, ex-

TIP: WINTERIZING IN COLD CLIMATES

Close the valve for the outdoor supply pipe, then remove the cap on the drain nipple. With the faucet on the outdoor spigot open, attach an air compressor to the valve nipple, then blow water from the system, using no more than 50 psi of air pressure. Remove the plugs from the tee fittings in each valve box, and store them for the winter.

tending the pipe through the hole in the bucket and out into the valve box.

4. Place the bucket and post in the hole, with the pipe extending into the valve box. Fill the bucket with concrete. Use a level to make sure the post is plumb.

Step E: Connect the Supply Line to the Spigot

1. Install a barbed tee fitting with a threaded outlet, opening facing down, to the PE pipe inside the valve box. Cap the threaded opening with a plug.

2. Using male and female threaded adapters, join the copper pipe to the PE pipe.

3. Repeat steps 1 and 2 to join the pipes in the valve box located near the house. Restore the water and test the line for leaks. Make any necessary adjustments, then refill the trenches. Replace the sod, tamp it down with a shovel, and water it thoroughly.

C. Lay a run of PE pipe along the bottom of the trench, joining sections with stainless steel clamps and insert couplings.

D. Attach the copper riser and spigot to the post. Place post in the bucket and fill it with concrete.

E. Inside the valve boxes, install a barbed PVC tee fitting with plug to the PE pipe. Join the copper and PE pipe with adapters.

Garden GFCI Receptacle

Even if your home already has a few exterior electrical receptacles, you can benefit from running at least one more GFCI receptacle to a garden location. A GFCI can be added to any outdoor room to help with a variety of tasks, including operating power tools, recharging battery-operated yard tools, powering a fountain or operating low-voltage lighting.

The following sequence illustrates a basic method for creating a freestanding receptacle anchored to a wood post embedded in a bucket of concrete. The receptacle is wired with UF (underground feeder) cable running through a trench from a junction box inside your house or garage. Sections of conduit protect the outdoor cable where it's exposed.

If you'd like to attach the outlet to an existing landscape structure, such as a deck or fence, you can modify the project by attaching the receptacle box and conduit to that structure. Keep in mind that freestanding receptacles should be at least 12", but no more than 18", above ground level.

Before you begin this project, have your local inspector review your plans and issue a work permit. Inspectors rely on the National Electrical Code (NEC) as well as local Codes that address climate and soil conditions in your region. If local Code requires that your work be inspected, schedule these visits at the appropriate points during the project.

TOOLS & MATERIALS

- Basic tools (page 16)
- Wire cutters
- Utility knife
- Fish tape
- Wire strippers
- LB connector
- Metal sweeps

- 1" metal conduit (6 ft.)
- Compression fittings
- Plastic bushings
- Pipe straps
- 2-gallon bucket
- 4-ft. 4 × 4 post

- Metal outdoor receptacle box
- Concrete mix
- UF cable
- GFCI receptacle
- Wire connectors
- Cable staples
- Grounding pigtail

HOW TO INSTALL A GARDEN RECEPTACLE
Step A: Plan the Route & Dig the Trench
1. Plan a convenient route from an accessible indoor junction to the location you've chosen for the GFCI.
   Drill a 1"-diameter hole through the exterior wall, near the junction box.

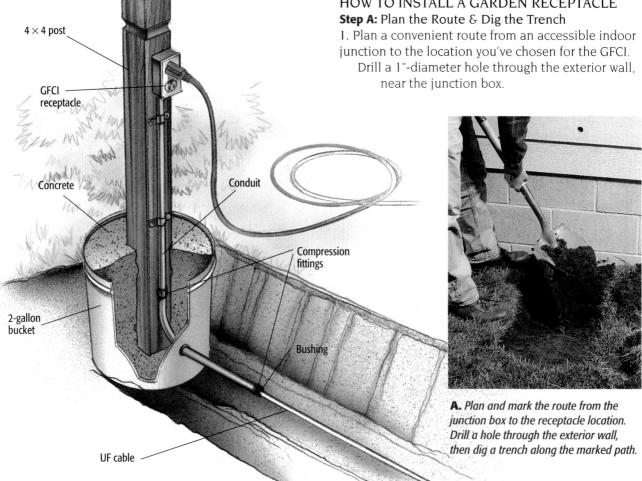

4 × 4 post

GFCI receptacle

Concrete

Conduit

Compression fittings

2-gallon bucket

Bushing

UF cable

A. Plan and mark the route from the junction box to the receptacle location. Drill a hole through the exterior wall, then dig a trench along the marked path.

2. Mark the underground cable run from the hole in the wall to the location for the receptacle.

3. Remove sod for an 8"- to 12"-wide trench along the marked route. Dig a trench that's at least 12" deep.

Step B: Install the LB Connector & Conduit

1. Install the LB connector on the outside of the hole.

2. Measure and cut a length of conduit about 4" shorter than the distance from the LB connector to the bottom of the trench. Attach the conduit to a sweep fitting, using a compression fitting. Attach a plastic bushing to the open end of the sweep to keep the sweep's metal edges from damaging the cable.

3. Attach the conduit assembly to the bottom of the LB connector, then anchor the conduit to the wall, using pipe straps.

4. Cut a short length of conduit to extend from the LB connector through the wall to the inside of the house. Attach the conduit to the LB connector from the inside of the house, then attach a plastic bushing to the open end of the conduit.

Step C: Assemble & Install the Receptacle Post

1. Drill or cut a 1½" hole through the side of a 2-gallon plastic bucket, near the bottom.

2. Mount the receptacle box to the post with galvanized screws. Position the post in the bucket.

3. Measure and cut a length of conduit to run from the receptacle box to a point 4" above the base of the

CHOOSING CABLE SIZES

This chart will help you determine what size UF cable you'll need to buy for this project.

Circuit Size	Circuit Length	Cable Gauge
15-amp	Less than 50 ft.	14
15-amp	More than 50 ft.	12
20-amp	Less than 50 ft.	12
20-amp	More than 50 ft.	10

bucket. Attach the conduit to the receptacle box and mount it to the post with pipe straps.

4. Insert a conduit sweep through the hole in the bucket and attach it to the end of the conduit, using a compression fitting. Thread a plastic bushing onto the open end of the sweep.

5. Dig a hole at the end of the trench. Place the bucket with the post into the hole, then fill the bucket with concrete and let it dry completely.

Step D: Lay the UF Cable

1. Measure the distance from the junction box in the house out to the receptacle box. Cut a length of UF cable 2 ft. longer than this measurement. At each end of the cable, use a utility knife to pare away 8" of the outer sheathing (page 49).

2. Lay the cable along the bottom of the trench from

B. Mount the LB connector over the hole in the wall. Assemble a length of conduit and sweep fitting.

C. Assemble and attach the receptacle box and conduit to the post, then position the assembly at the end of the trench and fill the bucket with concrete.

D. Measure and cut UF cable and lay it in the trench. Use a fish tape to pull the cable up into the LB connector.

Garden GFCI Receptacle (cont.)

the house to the receptacle location.

3. Open the cover on the LB connector and feed a fish tape down through the conduit and out of the sweep. Feed the wires at the end of the UF cable through the loop in the fish tape, then wrap electrical tape around the wires up to the sheathing.

4. Using the fish tape, carefully pull the end of the cable up through the conduit to the LB connector.

Step E: Fishing the UF Cable into the Receptacle Box

1. At the other end of the trench, feed the fish tape down through the conduit and out of the sweep.

2. Attach the exposed wires to the loop in the fish tape, and secure them with electrical tape.

3. Pull the cable through the conduit up into the receptacle box. About ½" of cable sheathing should extend into the box.

Step F: Connect the GFCI Receptacle

1. Using wire strippers, remove ¾" of the wire insulation around the two insulated wires extending into the receptacle box (opposite page).

2. Attach a bare copper pigtail to the grounding terminal on the back of the receptacle box. Join the two bare copper wires to the green grounding lead attached to the GFCI, using a wire connector.

3. Connect the black circuit wire to the brass screw terminal marked LINE on the GFCI. Connect the white wire to the silver terminal marked LINE.

4. Carefully tuck all the wires into the receptacle box, then mount the receptacle. Install the cover plate.

Step G: Connect the Cable at the Junction Box

1. From inside the house, extend the fish tape through the conduit and LB connector. Attach the cable wires to the fish tape, then pull the cable into the house.

2. Anchor the cable along framing members to the junction box, using wire staples.

3. **Turn off the power to the circuit serving the junction box.** Remove the junction box cover.

4. Use a screwdriver to open a knockout in the side of the junction box. Pull the end of the UF cable into the box through the knockout, and secure it with a cable clamp. About ½" of the outer sheathing should extend into the box, and the individual wires should be about 8" long. (Cut excess wire down to size.)

5. Using a wire stripper, remove ¾" of the wire insulation from the insulated wires (opposite page).

6. Unscrew the wire connector attached to the bare copper grounding wires inside the box. Position the new grounding wire alongside the existing wires and replace the wire connector.

7. Using the same technique, connect the new black wire to the existing black wires, and connect the new white wire to the existing white wires.

8. Replace the junction box cover and restore the power to the circuit. Fill the trench.

E. *Using the fish tape, pull the cable through the conduit and up into the receptacle box.*

F. *Connect the GFCI by joining the grounding wires with a wire connector and connecting the black wire to the brass LINE terminal, the white wire to the silver LINE terminal.*

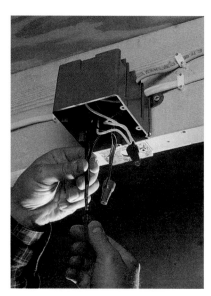

G. *Extend the UF cable into the juction box. Connect the new wires to the existing wires, using wire connectors.*

VARIATION: WIRING INTO AN EXISTING RECEPTACLE

Instead of wiring your garden GFCI into a junction box, you can wire it into an existing receptacle in your basement or garage. Before you begin, turn off the power to the existing receptacle.

1. Remove the cover plate and the receptacle. Loosen the mounting screws and remove the receptacle box.

2. Open a knockout in the side of the receptacle box with a screwdriver. Pull the end of the UF cable into the box through the knockout and secure it with a cable clamp.

3. Detach the circuit wires connected to the receptacle. Connect a bare copper pigtail to the ground screw terminal on the receptacle, a white pigtail to a silver screw terminal and a black pigtail to a brass screw terminal.

4. Using a wire connector for each set of wires, join the bare copper grounding wires, then the white neutral wires, then the black hot wires.

5. Carefully tuck the wires and receptacle back into the box. Replace the cover plate and restore the power.

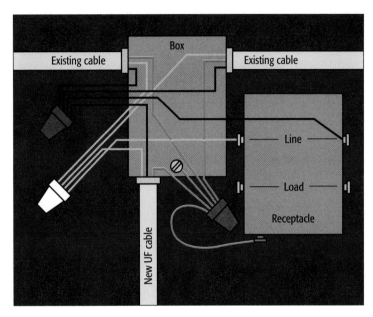

Box

Existing cable

Existing cable

Line

Load

Receptacle

New UF cable

TIP: BASIC WIRING SKILLS AND TECHNIQUES

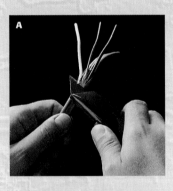

A. Stripping UF Cable Sheathing

Measure and cut a length of UF cable. At each end of the cable, use a utility knife to pare away 8" of the outer sheathing, using a technique similar to whittling a stick. Be careful not to nick or cut the wire insulation around the wires underneath.

B. Removing Wire Insulation

Strip ¾" of the insulation from each wire in the cable, using the wire stripper openings on a combination tool. Choose the opening that matches the gauge of the wire, then clamp the wire in the tool. Pull the wire firmly to remove the insulation. Take care not to nick or scratch the ends of the wires.

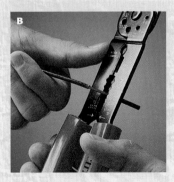

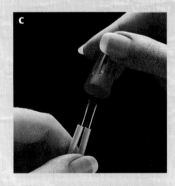

C. Connecting Two or More Wires

Hold the wires parallel, then screw a wire connector onto the wires. Tug gently on each wire to make sure it's secure. The wire connector cap should completely cover the bare wires.

Floodlight

Floodlights provide illumination for outdoor spaces frequently used at night, such as barbecue areas, basketball courts or garage entrances. In addition, floodlights improve your home's security.

In this project, we'll show you how to mount a motion-sensor floodlight on your garage. The light and its switch are wired into an existing GFCI receptacle located inside the garage.

Before you begin this project, draw a plan of your floodlight circuit and consult an inspector about local Code requirements. You'll also need to apply for a work permit with your local inspection office. If your Building Code requires inspections, make sure to have your work checked at the prescribed times.

TOOLS & MATERIALS

- Basic tools (page 16)
- Jig saw
- Cable ripper
- Wire combination tool
- Plastic light fixture box
- Plastic switch box
- 14-gauge NM cable
- Cable staples
- Floodlight with hardware
- Wire connectors
- Single pole switch

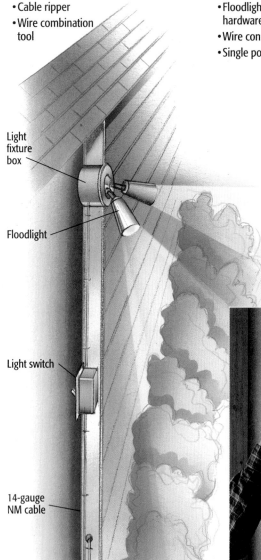

Light fixture box

Floodlight

Light switch

14-gauge NM cable

GFCI receptacle

HOW TO INSTALL A FLOODLIGHT

Step A: Install the Light Fixture Box

1. Turn off the power to the circuit that operates the receptacle to which you'll be wiring the floodlight.
2. Position the light fixture box against the inside sheathing of the garage wall, adjacent to a stud. Outline the box on the sheathing, then drill a pilot hole and complete the cutout with a jig saw.
3. Position the box so its edges extend into the cutout, then attach it to the stud by hammering in the premounted nails.

Step B: Mount the Switch Box & Run the Cable

1. Position the switch box against the side of a stud inside the garage, located near a GFCI receptacle.
2. Attach the box to the stud by hammering in the premounted nails at the top and bottom of the box.
3. Cut one length of cable to run from the light fixture box to the switch box, with an extra 1 ft. at each end. Anchor the cable to framing members (within 8" of the boxes), using cable staples.

A. Mark and cut the hole for the plastic light fixture box, then mount the box.

B. Attach the switch box to the side of a stud near a source GFCI receptacle. Run NM cable between the boxes.

4. Cut another length of cable to run from the switch box to the receptacle box, allowing an extra 1 ft. at each end. Anchor it with cable staples.

5. Strip away 10" of outer sheathing from both ends of each new cable, using a cable ripper. Strip away ¾" of insulation from each of the insulated wires, using a combination tool (see page 49).

Step C: Wire the Floodlight

1. Open a knockout in the light fixture box, using a screwdriver. Insert the new cable into the box through the knockout opening, so that about ½" of the cable sheathing extends into the box.

2. Assemble the light fixture according to manufacturer's instructions. Attach a bare copper grounding wire to the grounding screw on the light fixture.

3. From outside the garage, join the circuit grounding wire and the light fixture grounding wire with a wire connector. Using the same technique, connect the white circuit wire to the white fixture wire. Then, connect the black circuit wire and black fixture wire.

4. Carefully tuck the wires into the box, and attach the light fixture faceplate to the fixture box.

Step D: Wire the Switch

1. Open a knockout in the top and bottom of the switch box, using a screwdriver. Insert the new cables into the box through the knockouts, so about ½" of the cable sheathing extends into the box.

2. Attach a bare copper grounding pigtail to the grounding screw on the switch, then connect the copper pigtail and the two bare copper circuit grounding wires, using a wire connector.

3. Attach the black wire leading from the GFCI to one of the screw terminals on the switch. Attach the black wire leading to the light fixture to the other screw terminal. Connect the two white neutral wires together, using a wire connector.

4. Tuck the wires inside the switch box. Secure the switch inside the box, then install the faceplate.

Step E: Connect to the GFCI Receptacle

1. Make sure the power to the GFCI is turned off. Remove the cover from the source GFCI, then gently pull the receptacle from the box and detach the wires.

2. Open a knockout in the box, using a screwdriver, and insert the new cable, so that about ½" of the cable sheathing extends into the receptacle box.

3. Join the grounding pigtail on the GFCI to both circuit grounding wires, using a wire connector.

4. Attach the white wire entering the box from the power source to the silver GFCI screw terminal marked LINE. Attach the black wire from the power source to the brass screw terminal marked LINE.

5. Attach the white wire running from the box to the switch to the silver GFCI screw terminal marked LOAD. Attach the black wire leading to the switch to the brass screw terminal marked LOAD.

6. Tuck all wires back inside the box and carefully force the receptacle into the box and secure it with mounting screws. Install the cover; restore the power.

C. *Attach the wires on the light fixture to the corresponding circuit wires, using wire connectors.*

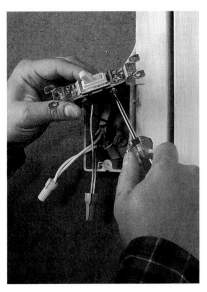

D. *Attach the black wires to the screw terminals on the switch. Join the white wires and the grounding wires together.*

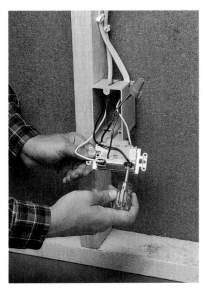

E. *Attach the wires from the power source to the LINE terminals and the circuit wires to the LOAD terminals.*

Landscape Lighting

Landscape lighting allows you to extend the use of your outdoor rooms well into the twilight hours, increases the security of your home and helps you safely navigate outdoor stairs and pathways at night. In addition, well-designed outdoor lighting transforms your landscape's appearance in the evening hours. The shapes, colors and textures of landscape elements are emphasized in new and striking ways.

The easiest way to add lighting to your outdoor rooms is with low-voltage lighting, available at home centers and garden supply stores. These outdoor lights are made of plastic or metal in a variety of styles that produce different effects. Several manufacturers have created modular kits that allow you to choose several styles of lights and the appropriate size power pack to operate them.

DESIGNING LOW-VOLTAGE LIGHTING

If possible, plan and install landscape lighting before you complete the planting areas. But if this isn't possible, carefully dig trenches and bury the lighting cable. When planning your lighting design, keep in mind that the most effective landscape lighting designs are created with a "less is more" philosophy. Overlighting, which is a common mistake, can make the landscape less inviting and disturb the neighbors. Good lighting designs focus on the glow of the lights and the illuminated objects, not the bulbs and fixtures. To achieve this effect, selectively position lights in unobtrusive places, such as garden beds, the eaves of a pergola, behind shrubs or even shining down from tree branches.

The illuminated objects and the glow of the lights, rather than the fixtures, are the focus of good landscape lighting designs.

Begin planning your lighting by touring your yard at night with a map of your landscape in hand. On your map, note the areas that need to be illuminated for safety or security reasons. Stairs, pathways, entrances, driveways and garages often require additional light. Also, consider which outdoor rooms you'd like to use at night and for what activities. For example, entertaining on a deck requires lighting for safety and convenience.

"Shadow lighting" casts the shadow of an interesting object onto a fence or wall that is directly behind the object.

Next, note attractive garden features you'd like to highlight in the evening hours: interesting trees and shrubs, sculptures, flower beds or water gardens make a striking impression when lighted. In addition, look for architectural features, such as walls, arbors, trellises and gates, that will create interesting patterns of light and shadow.

Once you've noted the areas you'd like to highlight, determine the best way to illuminate each area. You may want to use some of the following methods suggested by professional landscape designers.

Backlighting: Highlights an object from behind, creating a silhouette that stands out from the background. This technique is especially effective with lacy shrubs and solitary objects.

Shadow lighting: Directs a single beam of light on a specific object that has a wall or fence behind it, creating a shadow of the featured object. This technique works best for objects with interesting shapes.

"Uplighting" is achieved with floodlights or well lights, positioned to shine directly up at an object. Use uplighting to highlight trees, walls or outdoor sculpture.

Moonlighting: Places several spotlights in a tree or large overhead structure and directs the light downward to simulate the effect of moonlight.

Spotlighting: Emphasizes an interesting architectural or landscape feature with one or more direct beams of light.

Uplighting: Highlights trees, shrubs or architectural features with well lights or floodlights hidden directly below the featured object, creating a dramatic effect with light and shadow.

Grazing: Focuses a broad beam of light on the high point of a wall or fence and indirectly lights the lower portion of the structure, emphasizing the texture of the surface and the low shadows.

Sidelighting: Lights a pathway, stairway or another surface with a series of small, horizontally mounted spotlights.

"Sidelighting" uses a series of small, horizontally mounted spotlights to light a surface.

LIGHTING DESIGN TIP:

Place waterproof lights below the surface of the water to light water features, such as fountains and garden ponds. The lights shining up from the bottom make the water shimmer.

Low-voltage Lighting

Low-voltage lighting systems are a popular choice for landscape lighting because they're adaptable, easy to install and use little energy. Most outdoor lighting systems consist of the fixtures and bulbs, low-voltage connector cable, cable connector caps and a control box containing the power transformer, timer and light sensor. The control box for a low-voltage lighting system plugs into a standard outlet and uses standard 120-volt house current.

TOOLS & MATERIALS

- Basic tools (page 16)
- Trenching spade
- Ruler
- Low-voltage control box
- Low-voltage cable
- Outdoor-grade PVC conduit
- Pipe straps with screws
- Low-voltage lights
- Connector caps

HOW TO INSTALL LOW-VOLTAGE LIGHTING

Step A. Mount the Control Box

1. Mount the control box on an outside wall, close to a GFCI receptacle. Position the control box so that the sensor isn't covered by plants or other materials.
2. Slide the ends of the cables over the extended tabs on the base of the control box.
3. Dig a narrow trench for the light cable, about 6" to 8" deep. Start directly beneath the control box and extend the trench about 1 ft. out from the wall.
4. Measure the distance down from the base of the control box to the bottom of the trench. Cut a section of outdoor-grade PVC conduit to this length.
5. Feed the cable through the conduit, then position the conduit against the wall, with its bottom resting in the trench. Secure the conduit to the wall, using pipe straps.

Step B. Lay Out the Cable

Starting at the end of the conduit, lay out the cable along the ground. Since you'll need to bury the cable, select a path with few obstacles.

Step C. Attach the Light Fixtures

1. Beginning with the location closest to the control box, assemble the fixture you've picked for that spot.

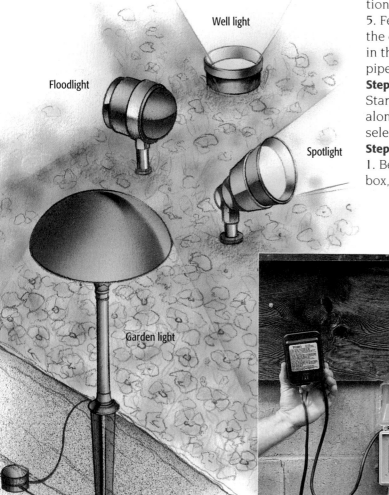

Well light

Floodlight

Spotlight

Garden light

B. Lay out the cable following the path you planned in your lighting design plan.

A. Mount the control box on an outside wall, close to a GFCI receptacle.

First, screw the bulb into the socket, then attach the lens and the hood to the fixture.

2. Carefully position the fixture, then firmly press its stake into the ground, in essence, planting the fixture.

3. Attach the fixture to the cable with a cable connector cap. Tighten the connector cap according to the manufacturer's directions, piercing the cable.

4. Repeat these steps to assemble, attach and position the remaining lights in your design.

Step D. Check & Adjust the Fixtures

Turn the lights on and survey your design. Look at the lights from several different directions and different areas of your yard, particularly from seating areas, to make sure that none of the lights produces a harsh glare or shines directly into your eyes. Adjust the fixtures as needed. If necessary, unfasten the connector cap, relocate a fixture, then reconnect it to the cable in its new location.

Step E. Dig a Trench & Bury the Cable

1. Beginning at the trench beneath the control box, dig a narrow trench, about 6" to 8" deep, along the cable path. At each fixture location, make a perpendicular slice with the spade to create a place to bury the section of cable leading to the fixture.

2. Gently push the cable into the bottom of the trench, using a wood or plastic ruler.

3. Replace the soil in the trenches and gently tamp it down with a spade.

VARIATION: LOW-VOLTAGE LIGHTING KIT

Home centers and garden supply stores carry a variety of low-voltage lighting products. Low-voltage outdoor light styles, like these from Toro®, include well lights (A), garden lights (B), adjustable spotlights (C) and adjustable floodlights (D). You'll also need low-voltage cable (E), halogen bulbs (F) and a control box (G), containing a transformer, timer and a light sensor to operate your light system.

C. Attach the fixture to the cable, using a cable connector cap.

D. Turn on the lights and survey the system from several areas, making adjustments as needed.

E. Cut a narrow trench along the cable path, then gently install the cable and close the trench.

Walls & Ceilings

Landscape walls and ceilings can increase privacy, improve home security, provide shade and diffuse strong winds. They also add interest by introducing new colors and textures, and by framing an attractive view or blocking an undesirable one. Walls often are installed along property lines, but can be used to define boundaries between rooms as well. Outdoor rooms also can be defined by ceilings, which offer the additional advantage of protecting a room and its contents from harsh sun or driving rain.

Walls and ceilings for an outdoor home can be created with nonliving materials, such as lumber and cut stone, or living materials, such as shrubs and trees.

Structures made from nonliving materials are generally easy to build and maintain, and provide attractive backdrops for decorative plantings and other landscape features. Wood, a relatively inexpensive material, is the most common choice for walls in today's outdoor homes. Wood fences are popular because they're attractive, easy to build and can be adapted to suit almost any landscape. Stone, another nonliving material, has a timeless appeal that blends well with almost any style of yard or garden. Building mortared walls may require more skill and experience than the average do-it-yourselfer possesses, but it's easy to create a beautiful, sturdy stone wall without mortar, using a technique known as dry laying.

Structures made of living materials contribute color, shape and texture to the landscape. For many people, the natural beauty of living materials more than offsets the routine care and maintenance they require. By using simple professional planting techniques, you can create anything from a tightly spaced, formal hedge to one that meanders gracefully across the contours of your yard.

IN THIS CHAPTER:

Walls

Fence

Fences establish visual boundaries and define spaces. A wood fence is one of the easiest and least expensive landscape walls you can build. A board-and-stringer fence, such as the one described here, is ideal for flat or sloped yards.

A fence is as much a part of your neighbors' landscape as your own. That's why local Building Codes often include restrictions on building fences. To avoid problems and misunderstandings, check local Building Codes and talk with your neighbors as you begin planning your project.

Before laying out fence lines, determine the exact property boundaries. It's a good idea to position the fence at least 6" inside your property line, even if Building Codes don't specify setback rules. The finished side of the fence should face out, with the exposed posts and stringers on the inside.

A board-and-stringer fence is constructed from a basic frame with at least two rails, called *stringers*, that run parallel to the ground. Stringers are attached to posts secured in concrete footings. Vertical boards, called *pickets*, are attached to the stringers.

Our version of a board-and-stringer fence is built with cedar lumber. It includes a gate, which provides access to the yard without sacrificing privacy or security. For convenience, we've used a prefabricated gate, which you can find at most home centers.

To ensure sturdy construction, the bases of our fence posts are buried in concrete footings. Remember that footing depths are determined by your local Building Code and keep this in mind when determining the lengths of your posts.

TOOLS & MATERIALS

- Basic tools (page 16)
- Stakes & string
- Line level
- Masking tape
- Plumb bob
- Posthole digger
- Reciprocating saw
- Circular saw
- Paintbrush
- Gravel
- 4 × 4 posts
- Concrete mix
- 6-ft. 2 × 4 lumber
- Wood sealer/protectant
- Galvanized screws (2½", 2", 1")
- 2" fence brackets
- 6d galvanized nails
- 1 × 6 lumber
- Prefabricated gate & hardware

HOW TO BUILD A FENCE

Step A: Mark the Post Locations

1. Mark the fence line with stakes and mason's string. Attach a line level to the string, then adjust the string on the stakes until it's level.

2. Find the on-center spacing of

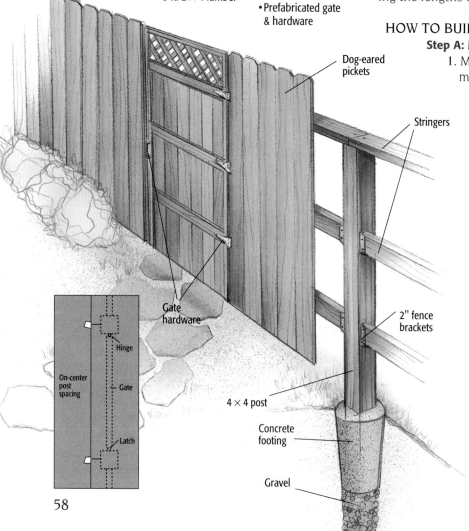

Dog-eared pickets

Stringers

2" fence brackets

4 × 4 post

Concrete footing

Gravel

Gate hardware

On-center post spacing

Hinge

Gate

Latch

A. *Mark the fence line with a pair of stakes and a leveled string, then mark the location of the gate and posts.*

58

the gate posts by measuring the gate width, including hinge and latch hardware, and adding 4". Place masking tape on the string to mark the location of the gate posts.

3. Use tape to mark the string with the remaining post locations, spacing them 6 ft. apart on center.

4. Pinpoint the post locations on the ground, using a plumb bob. Mark post locations with stakes, and remove the string from the fence line markers.

Step B: Set the Posts

1. Seal the portions of posts that will be buried and let them dry.

2. Dig the postholes, using a posthole digger or a power auger. Make the holes 6" deeper than the post footing depth specified by your local Building Code.

3. Pour a 6" layer of gravel into each hole.

4. Place each post in its hole, then use a level to plumb the post. Brace the post in place with scrap pieces of 2 × 4 driven into the ground and screwed to the sides of the post on adjoining faces.

5. When all of the posts are braced in position, use the mason's string to make sure they are in a straight line. Make adjustments as needed.

Step C: Pour the Footings

1. Mix concrete in a wheelbarrow, and fill the holes, slightly overfilling and tamping each one.

2. Check the posts with a level to be sure they're plumb, then shape the concrete to form a mound that will shed water away from the post.

VARIATION: FENCE PANELS

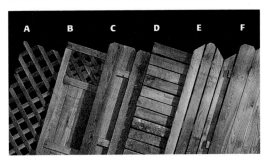

Preassembled fence panels are an attractive, timesaving option when building a fence. The entire panel is attached to the posts, eliminating the need to individually cut and attach stringers.

Some popular styles of prefabricated panels include:

A. Lattice panels
B. Solid panels with lattice tops
C. Staggered board
D. Horizontal board
E. Modified picket
F. Dog-eared board

3. Let the concrete dry for at least 24 hours before continuing with the fence installation.

Step D: Trim the Posts & Add the Top Stringers

1. On each end post, measure up from the ground to a point 1 ft. below the planned height of the fence. Snap a chalk line across all the posts at this height. Trim the posts to height with a reciprocating saw, making sure these cuts are square.

B. *Position each post in its hole. Adjust the post until it's plumb, then brace it with 2 × 4 cross braces driven into the ground.*

C. *Fill the holes with concrete. Recheck the posts for plumb, then shape the concrete into a raised cap.*

D. *Trim the posts, and place the cut stringers on top of the posts, with the joints centered. Attach with screws.*

Fence (cont.)

2. Cut 6-ft. 2 × 4 stringers and coat the ends with sealer. Let the sealer dry.

3. Place the stringers flat on top of the posts, centering a joint over each post. Attach the stringers to the posts with 2½" galvanized screws.

Step E: Install the Remaining Stringers

1. Measuring down from the top of each post, mark lines at 2-ft. intervals to mark the locations for the remaining stringers. At each mark, nail a 2" fence bracket to the side of the post, flush with the outside edge.

2. Position a 2 × 4 stringer between each pair of brackets. Hold or tack the board against the posts, and mark the back side, along the edges of the posts. (If the yard slopes, the stringers will be cut at an angle.)

3. Cut the stringers ¼" shorter than indicated, which will help them slide into the brackets easily. Coat the cut ends of the stringers with sealer/protectant.

4. If stringers are angled to accommodate a slope, bend the bottom flanges of the brackets to match the angles of the stringers. Position and nail the stringers into place, using 6d galvanized nails.

Step F: Attach the Pickets

1. Install the pickets, beginning at an end post. Measure from the ground to the top edge of the top

TIP:

Instead of digging the postholes with a post-hole digger, you can use a rented power auger to make the job faster and less strenuous.

stringer, then add 8½". Cut a picket to this length. Coat the bottom edge of the picket with sealer/protectant.

2. Position the picket so that the top extends 10½" above the top stringer, leaving a 2" gap at the bottom. Make sure the picket is plumb, then attach it to the post and rails with pairs of 2" galvanized screws.

3. Measure, cut and attach the remaining pickets to the stringers, using the same procedure. Leave a gap of at least ⅛" between boards, using a piece of scrap wood as a spacing guide. At the ends of the fence, you may need to rip-cut pickets to make them fit.

Step G: Hang the Gate

1. Attach three hinges, evenly spaced, to the gate frame. Make sure the hinges are parallel with the edge of the gate.

2. Position the gate upright between the gate posts, resting the hinge barrels against the face of the fence. Support the gate on wood blocks at the correct height, then attach the hinges to the fence.

3. On the opposite side, attach the latch hardware to the fence and to the gate. Open and close the gate to make sure the latch works correctly, then make any adjustments that are necessary.

4. Coat the fence completely with sealer/protectant.

E. *Attach the fence brackets to the inside faces of the posts. Position the stringers in the brackets, then nail them in place.*

F. *Measure and cut the pickets. Attach them to the posts and stringers, spacing the pickets at least ⅛" apart.*

G. *Attach the hinges according to the manufacturer's directions, then hang the gate and install latch hardware.*

VARIATION: FENCES

A. Combining materials modifies the total effect. The formality of these brick pillars is softened by the openness of the wood fence.

B. Chain-link fences are economical and sturdy. To help integrate them into the landscape, plant climbing vines, such as this clematis.

C. Brick fences lend an air of solidity and permanence to a landscape. Here, repeated materials result in a pleasing balance.

D. Details, such as the cutouts shown on the pickets above, can be used to create unique variations of standard fence styles.

E. A split-rail fence is an inexpensive, easy-to-build option that works best in rustic or informal landscapes.

Stone Wall

Stone walls are beautiful, long-lasting structures that add an elegant touch to any landscape. Surprisingly, they're simple to build. A low stone wall can be constructed without mortar, using a centuries-old method known as "dry laying." With this technique, the wall is actually formed by two separate stacks that lean together slightly. The position and weight of the two stacks support each other, forming a single, sturdy wall. A dry stone wall can be built to any length, but must be at least half as wide as it is tall.

The best place to purchase stone for this project is from a quarry or aggregate supply center. These centers sell different sizes, shapes and colors of stone, each type priced by the ton. For a dry stone wall,

you'll need to purchase stone in four sizes:
• Shaping: ½" the width of the wall
• Tie: the same width as the wall
• Filler: small shims that fit into cracks
• Cap: large, flat stones, wider than the wall

While dry walls are simple to construct, they do require a fair amount of patience. The stones must be carefully selected and sorted by size and shape. Some may also need to be shaped or split to maintain the spacing and structure of the wall.

To shape a stone, score its surface, using a circular saw outfitted with a masonry blade. Place a mason's chisel on the cut and strike it with a hand sledge until the stone breaks. Always wear safety glasses when cutting or shaping stone.

HOW TO BUILD A DRY STONE WALL

Step A: Dig the Trench
1. Sort the stones by size and purpose, placing them in piles near the building site.
2. Lay out the wall site, using stakes and string.
3. Dig a 2-ft.-wide trench, 4" to 6" deep, along the site, creating a slight "V" shape by sloping the sides toward the center. The center of the trench should be about 2" deeper than the sides.

Step B: Build the First Course
1. Select appropriate stones from the pile of shaping stones, and lay the first course along the bottom of the trench. Place pairs of stones side by side, flush

---

TOOLS & MATERIALS

- Basic tools (page 16)
- Stakes
- String
- Stone
- Circular saw with masonry blade
- Mason's chisel
- Mortar
- Masonry trowel

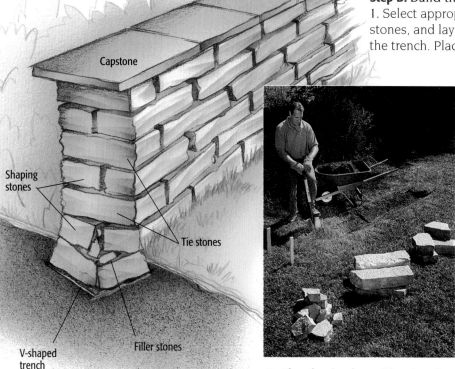

Capstone

Shaping stones

Tie stones

Filler stones

V-shaped trench

A. *After planning the wall location, dig a V-shaped trench for the wall. Sort the stones by size and purpose.*

B. *Lay the first course of shaping stones in the trench, adjusting them so that they slope toward each other.*

with the edges of the trench and sloping toward the center. As you position stones along the first course, use stones similar in height; if stones have uneven surfaces, position them with the uneven side facing down.

2. Fill any significant gaps between the shaping stones with filler stones.

Step C: Add the Second Course

1. Lay the second course of stones over the first, staggering the joints. If possible, use pairs of stones in varying lengths to offset the center joint.

2. Alternate the stones in a longer-shorter pattern. Keep the height of the second course even, stacking two thinner stones if necessary to maintain a consistent height.

3. Wedge filler stones into any large gaps.

Step D: Lay the Tie Stones

1. Following the same technique, lay the third course of shaping stones, placing a tie stone every 3 ft. To keep the tie stones uniform, you may need to cut them to length. Hold a level along the side of the wall periodically to check it for level.

2. Lay shaping stones between tie stones and continue placing filler stones into any cracks on the surface and sides of the wall.

Step E: Finish the Wall

1. Continue laying courses, maintaining a consistent height along the wall and adding tie stones to every third course.

TIP: MOVING STONES

To avoid injury, squat and lift heavy stones with the strength of your legs rather than your back.

Use a wheelbarrow for lifting and transporting heavy stones that are too large to carry. To load the stone, place the wheelbarrow on its side behind the stone, then roll the stone onto the edge.

Stand behind the wheelbarrow and use the strength of your legs to pull the wheelbarrow toward you until it's resting upright.

2. When the wall is approximately 4 ft. high, check it for level. When you're satisfied with the placement of stones, blind-mortar the capstones to the top of the wall. Using a trowel, apply mortar to the center of the wall, keeping the mortar at least 6" from the edges. Center the capstones over the wall, and set them as close together as possible.

3. Carefully fill the cracks between the capstones with mortar. Let any excess mortar dry until crumbly, then brush it off. After two or three days, scrub off any residue, using water and a rough-textured rag.

filler stones

C. Lay the second course of shaping stones over the first course, placing filler stones into the cracks as you work.

tie stones

D. Add the third course of stone over the second, using tie stones every 3 ft., checking periodically with a level.

E. Once all the courses are in place, mortar the capstones to the top course of stone, then seal the gaps between them.

Hedges

Hedges are a natural choice for creating landscape walls. Because hedges are a living wall of individual shrubs, they easily blend into any landscape. Like fences and other nonliving walls, hedges can take many forms, depending on the purpose and style you have in mind. For instance, an informal hedge of flowering shrubs adds seasonal color, while a formal hedge of closely planted evergreens forms a dense screen that increases privacy.

Shrub choices generally fall into two groups: fast-growing or steady-growing. Carefully consider the pros and cons of each before selecting shrubs for a hedge. Fast-growing shrubs quickly form a solid hedge, but their rapid growth makes it necessary to prune them frequently in order to keep the hedge well shaped and healthy. Steady-growing shrubs require less frequent pruning, but take at least several years to grow into a solid wall.

Local nurseries will have a selection of bare-root, balled-and-burlapped and container-grown shrubs. Because planting a hedge involves many shrubs, container-grown plants are the best choice—they usually are more economical and easier to transport and plant. If you decide to plant either bare-root or balled-and-burlapped shrubs, refer to the information on transporting and planting these types in "Trees" (page 66).

To ensure that the shrubs grow into a dense hedge, determine their mature size and space them at about ¾ of this measurement. Check with a nursery before you begin planting—some shrubs require different spacing. The size of the excavation also has a tremendous influence on the success of your hedge. In most cases, you'll want to dig a hole twice as wide and just as deep as the container. However, if you have heavy soil, dig a hole that will position the top of the root ball slightly above ground, then

TOOLS & MATERIALS

- Basic tools (page 16)
- Stakes
- String
- Rope or hose
- Soil amendments
- Shrubs
- Mulch

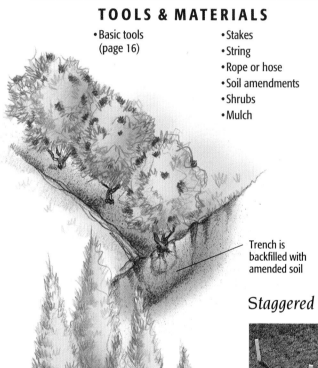

Trench is backfilled with amended soil

Planting hole is twice as wide and just as deep as the original container

Trenched

Staggered

Staggered Hedge

A. *Dig holes twice as wide and just as deep as the shrub's container, staggering the rows along both sides of the line.*

B. *After partially backfilling soil around the plant, water the soil. Finish filling the hole and apply a thick layer of mulch.*

mound the soil up to cover the roots.

Begin training the shrubs into a hedge by pruning them the first year. Taper the shrub so the bottom of the plant is wider than the top. Don't overprune—in general, it's best to prune within 2" of the last pruning.

HOW TO PLANT A STAGGERED HEDGE

The staggered planting method is the best choice for quickly forming an informal, living wall. It's also the preferred method if you're using shrubs that can't be planted close together. Although the hedge demonstrated here is straight, you can use a rope to lay out a curved hedge.

Step A: Dig Planting Holes
1. Use stakes and string to lay out the hedge's path.
2. On one side of the string, mark the appropriate spacing for a row of planting holes, then dig them.
3. On the other side of the string, mark and dig another row of holes, staggered with the first row.

Step B: Install the Plants
1. Center a plant in the hole, positioning it so the root ball is at the desired depth.
2. Fill the hole ¾ full with amended soil.
3. When the hole is ¾ full, slowly add water, which will remove any air pockets. Finish filling the hole with soil and tamp it gently.
4. Apply 4" to 6" of mulch and water the shrubs.

HOW TO PLANT A TRENCHED HEDGE

Another option for planting a hedge involves digging a trench. This trench method works best if you want a formal or shaped hedge, and if you are willing to wait for the plants to grow into a solid screen.

Step A: Dig the Trench
Outline the path for a curved hedge, using a rope. If you're planting a straight hedge, use stakes and string to mark the path. Dig a trench, twice as wide and just as deep as the shrubs' containers.

Step B: Install the Shrubs
Plant the shrubs one at a time, spacing them appropriately for their mature size. Hold each plant so it's centered and straight in the trench. Use the same planting technique described in the "Staggered Hedge" instructions, then apply mulch and water the shrubs generously.

TIP: PREPARING CONTAINER-GROWN SHRUBS FOR PLANTING

Container-grown shrubs and plants often become "root bound" in their containers and need to be prepared for planting. To prepare a container-grown plant, remove it from the container just before planting. Using a trowel, make vertical slices into the sides of the root ball, slicing through roots as necessary. Use the hand trowel to slice an "X" in the bottom of the root ball. This allows the roots to spread naturally as the plant grows.

Trenched Hedge

A. *Lay out the hedge path with a rope, then dig a trench twice the width and the same depth as the container.*

B. *Plant the shrubs one at a time, spacing them ¾ of their mature size apart. Fill the trench with soil.*

Trees

Trees help your landscape look more complete and add vertical interest to your yard. They also increase the value of the property and form natural landscape walls and ceilings. Planting trees in formation, similar to a hedge, creates a privacy screen, reduces noise and protects your house from strong winds. You can also plant a single tree that will, at mature height, form a graceful ceiling for one or more of your outdoor rooms.

SELECTING TREES

Nurseries and garden centers sell trees packaged in three different ways. Each packaging method has advantages and disadvantages.

Container-grown are packed in pots of soil and are available in many sizes.

Bare-root trees are dug up during dormancy, so the branches and roots are bare. The roots are exposed and must be kept moist and protected from sun and wind damage during transport and before planting.

Balled-and-burlapped (B & B) trees are established trees with a large compact root ball that's tightly secured in burlap. Balled-and-burlapped trees are very heavy, and require special care when transporting. The soil and roots must not dry out before planting.

TRANSPORTING TREES

All trees need protection during transport. Because this can be a difficult process, many people opt to pay the nursery a delivery fee to handle the job. But, if you have access to a pickup or trailer, you can save money by transporting the tree yourself. Branches, foliage and roots must be protected from breakage, and wind and sun damage, during transport. To protect them, wrap them in burlap tied on with twine. Secure the tree inside the truck bed with straps or rope. Drive slowly and carefully, especially on corners, and unload the tree by lifting it only by the roots, not the trunk.

HOW TO PREPARE THE PLANTING HOLE

The planting hole is one of the greatest contributing factors to the health of a tree. To prepare the hole, start by digging a hole two to three times as

Protect a tree during transport by wrapping the roots, branches and leaves with burlap, then securing it with heavy twine.

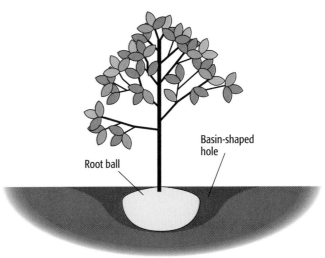

Root ball

Basin-shaped hole

wide as the root ball of the tree. If you're planting a bare-root tree, the hole should be two to three times wider than the spread of the branches. To help the roots develop horizontally, slope the sides of the hole toward the surface. When finished, the hole should resemble a wide, shallow basin.

HOW TO PLANT BARE-ROOT TREES

The roots of bare-root trees should be planted at a depth that is slightly higher than that at which they were originally grown. Start by slightly backfilling the planting hole with the soil you removed. Hold the tree in the hole; if the tops of the roots are still below the top of the hole, backfill more soil into the hole. Position the tree so that the largest branches are facing southwest, then spread out the roots. Backfill into the hole, covering the roots. As you backfill, gently lift the tree up and down to prevent air pockets from forming. When the hole is ¾ full, tamp the soil and water it generously to remove any remaining air pockets. Completely fill the hole with soil, and lightly tamp it.

HOW TO PLANT B & B TREES

Carefully set the plant in the hole. Add or remove soil until the root ball rests slightly above ground level. Cut and remove the twine at the top of the ball. Cut the burlap away from top and sides of the root-ball and remove as much of it as possible. Set the tree back down and backfill until the hole is ¾ full. Lightly tamp the soil down, then water it slowly to remove the air pockets. Finish backfilling the hole, and tamp the soil.

CARING FOR NEW TREES

Trees require routine maintenance—especially during the first year. It takes almost a full year for a newly planted tree to establish a healthy root system. During the root development period, routine waterings are very important.

The best method for watering trees is to place a garden hose adjusted to release water in a slow trickle at the base of the tree for several hours. With this method, you can easily water the soil around the tree to a depth of 6" to 8". Use this method to water new trees any time the moisture depth in the soil is less than 6". In addition to watering, encourage root development by applying a fertilizer formulated for trees, every two to three years. Apply the fertilizer according to the directions on the label.

Position bare-root trees so that the largest branches face southwest. Then spread the roots out in the soil before backfilling the planting hole.

(left) Cut and remove the twine from the top of balled-and-burlapped trees. Cut the burlap away, and remove it from around the tree.

(below) Trees are sold in several forms: bare root (A), container grown (B) and balled-and-burlapped (C).

A

B

C

67

2 × 2 cross strip

2 × 6 tie beam

2 × 4 rafters

4 × 4 post

Cement

Gravel

Arbor

TOOLS & MATERIALS

- Basic tools (page 16)
- Stakes and string
- Line level
- Posthole digger
- Reciprocating saw
- Paintbrush
- Wood screw clamps

- Concrete mix
- Gravel
- Wood sealer
- 10-ft. 4 × 4 posts (4)
- 6-ft. 2 × 6 tie beams (2)
- Galvanized nails

- 7-ft. 2 × 2 cross strips (7)
- 7-ft. 2 × 4 rafters (4)
- Galvanized deck screws
- 3" lag screws (8)
- Rafter ties (8)

Arbors create a lightly shaded space and add vertical interest to your landscape. For increased shade, you can cover an arbor with meshlike outdoor fabric or climbing vines. You can even transform it into a private retreat by enclosing the sides with lattice.

Our version of a post-and-slat arbor is a 5-ft. × 5-ft., freestanding cedar structure with an extended overhead. You can easily adapt the design to different sizes, but don't space the posts more than 8 ft. apart. If you want to build a larger arbor, add additional posts between the corner posts. Before you begin construction, check your local Building Code for footing depth requirements and setback restrictions.

If you want to add climbing vines, such as clematis or wisteria, plant one vine beside the base of each post. Attach screw eyes to the outside of the posts, then string wire between the eyes. As the vines grow, train them along the wires.

A. *Lay out the location of the arbor posts, then check the diagonals for squareness.*

B. *Brace the posts into place, then use a level to make sure they are plumb.*

C. *Level and clamp the tie beam against the posts, then secure it with lag screws.*

HOW TO BUILD AN ARBOR

Step A: Dig Holes for the Footings

1. Lay out the location of the posts, 5 ft. apart, using stakes and string. Make sure the layout is square by measuring from corner to corner and adjusting the layout until these diagonal measurements are equal.
2. Dig postholes at the corners to the required depth, using a posthole digger.
3. Fill each hole with 6" of gravel.

Step B: Set the Posts

1. Position the posts in the holes. To brace them in a plumb position, tack support boards to the posts on adjoining faces. Adjust the posts as necessary until they're plumb.
2. Drive a stake into the ground, flush against the base of each 2 × 4. Drive galvanized deck screws through the stakes, into the 2 × 4s.
3. Mix one bag of dry concrete to anchor each post. Immediately check to make sure the posts are plumb, and adjust as necessary until the concrete begins to harden. Be sure to let the concrete dry at least 24 hours before continuing.

Step C: Install the First Tie Beam

1. Measure, mark and cut all the lumber for the arbor. Cut a 3" × 3" notch off the bottom corner of each tie beam, a 2" × 2" notch off the bottom corner of each 2 × 4 rafter, and a 1" × 1" notch off the bottom corner of each cross strip.

2. Position a tie beam against the outside edge of a pair of posts, 7 ft. above the ground. Position the beam to extend about 1 ft. past the post on each side.
3. Level the beam, then clamp it into place with wood screw clamps. Drill two ⅜" pilot holes through the tie beam and into each post. Attach the tie beam to the posts with 3" lag screws.

Step D: Add the Second Tie Beam

1. Use a line level to mark the opposite pair of posts at the same height as the installed tie beam.
2. Attach the remaining tie beam, repeating the process described in #2 and #3 of Step C.
3. Cut off the posts so they're level with the tops of the tie beams, using a reciprocating saw or hand saw.

Step E: Attach the Rafters

Attach the rafters to the tops of the tie beams, using rafter ties and galvanized nails. Beginning 6" from the ends of the tie beams, space the rafters 2 ft. apart, with the ends extending past each tie beam by 1 ft.

Step F: Install the Cross Strips

1. Position a cross strip across the top of the rafters, beginning 6" from the ends of the rafters. Center the strip so it extends past the outside rafters by about 6". Drill pilot holes through the cross strip and into the rafters. Attach the cross strip with galvanized screws. Add the remaining cross strips, spacing them 1 ft. apart.
2. Finish your arbor by applying wood sealer.

D. *Attach the other tie beam and trim the tops of the posts flush with the tie beams.*

E. *Attach the rafters to the tie beams with rafter ties and galvanized nails.*

F. *Space the cross strips 1 ft. apart and attach them to the rafters.*

Floors

Of all the elements in your landscape, floors are perhaps the most important. By serving as a background for the rest of your landscape, outdoor flooring visually sets the tone for the yard. Carefully chosen flooring transforms a yard into a series of living spaces by providing a suitable surface for each room's intended purpose and activities.

By their nature, outdoor floors must withstand heavy use and the seasonal stress of the weather. You'll need to carefully select your materials, keeping in mind the style and purpose of the area as well as the climate in your region.

Grass is the most common outdoor floor covering, but there are a variety of other materials you can use. Brick, stone, concrete, wood and gravel can be used alone or in combination to create attractive, durable outdoor floors. Look for ways of repeating materials used elsewhere in your landscape or house. For example, if you have an attractive wood fence, use the same type of wood in a deck. Or if your home has a distinctive brick facade, repeat this element in a patio or walkway.

The flooring projects in this section illustrate the basics of paving with gravel, stone, brick, concrete and wood. With an understanding of these techniques, you can easily complete projects as demonstrated or create variations. Many of the projects include suggestions for other materials, applications or techniques you can apply to the basic principles.

Because there are many situations where a traditional carpet of healthy green grass works best, we've also demonstrated professional methods for starting a new lawn or renovating an existing lawn.

Floors

Surface Preparation

A well-constructed base is crucial to the success of any paving project. The quality of the base, which protects the paving project from time- and weather-inflicted damage, determines the longevity of the project. Whether you're building a stepping-stone path, a concrete patio or a brick walkway, surface preparation is vital to the success of your project.

The best material for a paving base is compactible gravel. The gravel is applied and compressed over evenly excavated soil, creating a smooth surface to pave. In addition, gravel drains water easily, preventing erosion and frost heave.

For most paving projects, it's best to cover the base with a layer of landscape fabric. The fabric prevents grass and weeds from growing up through the paving. Cut the landscape fabric into sheets and arrange them so that the edges overlap by 6". For some projects, you'll need to add a layer of sand over the landscape fabric.

The most important part of surface preparation is excavating and creating a smooth base with the proper slope for drainage. Before you begin excavating, evaluate the grade of the area you're paving, as shown in "Grading," (page 24). If the area is uneven or has a severe slope, you'll probably need to excavate or fill the area, then level it before you begin paving.

TOOLS & MATERIALS

- Basic tools (page 16)
- Line level
- Stakes
- String
- Compactible gravel
- Sod cutter (optional)
- Rented plate compactor or hand tamp

HOW TO PREPARE SURFACES FOR PAVING

Step A: Outline the Excavation Area

1. If you're paving a straight design, outline the area with stakes and string. Place the stakes so that they're at least 1 ft. outside the site the intersecting strings will mark—the actual corners of the paved surface. Use a line

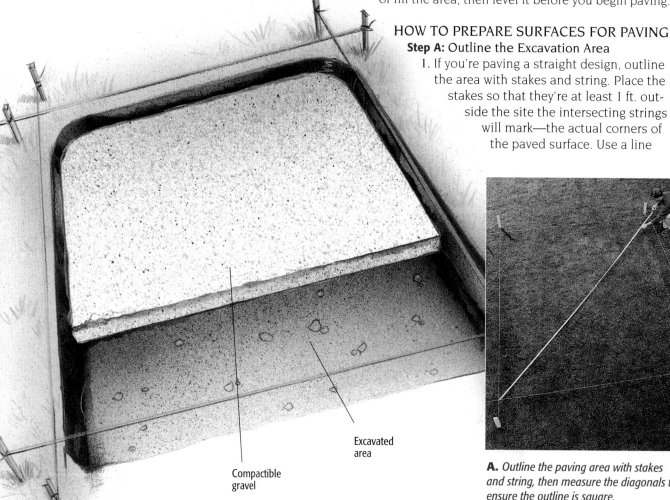

Excavated area

Compactible gravel

A. *Outline the paving area with stakes and string, then measure the diagonals to ensure the outline is square.*

level to level the strings. (For curves, use a rope or garden hose to lay out the design.)

2. Measure diagonally across the corners to make sure the outline is square. Adjust the stakes until these diagonal measurements are equal. For straight designs with rounded corners, as shown below, use a rope or garden hose to mark the curves.

Step B: Excavate the Area

1. Starting at the outside edge, use a shovel to evenly excavate the outlined area so it's about 5" deeper than the thickness of the planned paving.

2. Use a long 2 × 4 to check the surface for high and low spots, then redistribute soil as necessary to create a smooth, even surface across the entire area.

3. If you're building a paver patio or walkway, excavate 6" beyond the planned width and length of the project, which allows room for the edging.

Step C: Add Compactible Gravel

1. Pour compactible gravel over the excavated area, then rake it into a smooth layer at least 4" deep. The thickness of this base layer can vary to compensate for any unevenness in the excavation.

2. Use the 2 × 4 to check the surface once again for high and low spots, and add or remove gravel as needed to make the surface even.

Step D: Compact the Gravel

1. Use a rented plate compactor to pack the gravel

TIP: RENTING A SOD CUTTER

You may want to rent a sod cutter to strip grass from your pathway or patio site. Sod cutters, available at most rental centers, help you save time on big projects. These machines excavate at a very even depth, allowing you to roll up the removed sod. The cut sod can be replanted in other areas of your yard.

into a firm, even surface. For small areas, you can pack down the gravel with a hand tamp.

2. Check the evenness of the gravel base with a 2 × 4. Remove or add gravel as needed, then repack the base with the plate compactor.

B. Remove soil from the outlined layer with a shovel until the excavation is 5" deeper than the height of the paving.

C. Pour compactible gravel over the excavated area, then rake it into a smooth 4" layer.

D. Use a rented plate compactor (pictured) or a hand tamp to pack the gravel into a firm, flat surface.

73

Loose-fill Pathway

Walkways and paths serve as hallways between heavily used areas of your yard. In addition to directing traffic, paths create visual corridors that direct the eye to attractive features or areas.

A loose-fill pathway is a simple, inexpensive alternative to a concrete or paved path. Lightweight loose materials, such as gravel, crushed rock, bark or wood chips are used to "pave" a prepared pathway surface. Because the materials are not fixed within the path, edging is installed around the perimeter of the pathway to hold them in place. In addition to using standard preformed plastic edging, you can fashion edging from common hardscape building materials, such as wood, cut stone and brick pavers. For professional-looking re-

sults, repeat a material used in the exterior of the house or other landscape structures in the pathway edging. Select loose-fill materials that complement the color and texture of your edging.

Our loose-fill project uses brick edging set in soil, which works well for casual, lightly traveled pathways. However, this method should be used only in dense, well-drained soil. Bricks set in loose or swampy soil won't hold their position.

Loose-fill materials are available at most home and garden stores. Many stores sell these materials prebagged, which makes transporting and applying them easier. Aggregate supply companies also sell crushed rock and pea gravel in bulk, which is often a less expensive option. If you buy loose-fill material in bulk, it may be easier to have the supplier deliver it than to transport it yourself.

As you prepare to build a path, consider how it will normally be used, keeping in mind that loose-fill pathways are best suited to light-traffic areas. Also think about how the path will fit into the overall style and shape of your landscape. Curved pathways create a soft, relaxed look that complements traditional landscape designs, while straight or angular paths fit well in contemporary designs. You may want

TOOLS & MATERIALS

- Basic tools (page 16)
- Trenching spade
- Landscape fabric
- Rope
- Brick pavers
- Loose-fill material

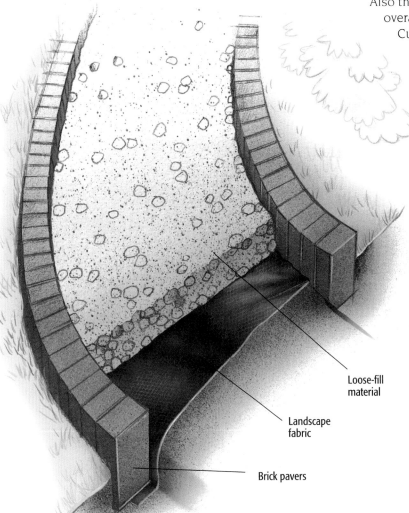

Loose-fill material

Landscape fabric

Brick pavers

A. *Dig narrow trenches for the edging on both sides of the excavated path site. Check the depth with a brick paver.*

to strategically place the path to lend depth to an area or highlight an interesting element.

HOW TO CREATE A LOOSE-FILL PATHWAY

Step A: Excavate the Path

1. Lay out the shape of the path with a rope or garden hose, then use a spade to excavate the area to a depth of 3". Rake the site smooth.

2. Dig narrow edging trenches along both edges of the path site, using a trenching spade or hoe. Make the trenches about 2" deeper than the path.

3. Test the trench depth with a brick paver placed on end in the trench—the top of the brick should stand several inches above ground. If necessary, adjust the trench to bring the bricks to the correct height.

Step B: Add Landscape Fabric

Line the trench with strips of landscape fabric, overlapping the strips by at least 6". Push the ends of the landscape fabric into the edging trenches.

Step C: Set the Bricks

1. Set the bricks into the edging trenches. Arrange them side by side, with no gaps between bricks.

2. Using a trowel, pack soil behind and beneath each brick. Adjust bricks as necessary to keep rows even.

Step D: Spread the Loose Fill

1. Spread the loose-fill material, adding material until it sits slightly above ground level. Level the

VARIATION: CHILDREN'S PLAY AREA

Using the same techniques shown here for building a path, you can pave the floor of an outdoor room with loose-fill material. Simply excavate and level the area, as shown in "Surface Preparation" (page 72).

Loose-fill paving, especially pea gravel or sand, works well in a children's play area.

surface, using a garden rake.

2. Tap the bricks lightly on the inside faces to help set them into the soil. Inspect and adjust the bricks yearly, adding new loose-fill material as necessary.

B. Place strips of landscape fabric over the path and into the edging trenches, overlapping sections by 6".

C. Install bricks end to end and flush against each other in the trenches, then pack soil behind and beneath each brick.

D. Fill the pathways with loose-fill material. Tap the inside face of each brick paver with a mallet to help set them permanently in the ground.

Stepping-stone Path

Whether you are paving a frequently traveled area, or introducing a sense of movement to your landscape, a stepping-stone path can be an ideal and inexpensive solution. A thoughtfully arranged stepping-stone design almost begs to be walked upon, and its open design complements, rather than overpowers, the landscape.

When designing your path, keep in mind that paths with gentle curves or bends are usually more attractive than straight ones. The distance between the stones is also an important consideration. Set the stones to accommodate a normal stride, so you can effortlessly step from one stone to the next.

There are a variety of materials available for constructing stepping-stone paths, from natural stone to prefabricated concrete. To ensure that your path blends with the rest or your landscape, select a material that suits your yard's style and existing materials. Natural stone indigenous to your area is often a good choice. Many stone yards sell 1" to 2½" sedimentary rock "steppers," which are ideal for stepping-stone paths. But you can also use cut stone, wood rounds or precast concrete pavers.

Even if you expect it to be more decorative than functional, keep safety in mind as you purchase materials and build your path. Select stones that are wide enough to stand on comfortably and have a flat, even, lightly textured surface.

Like other paved surfaces, stepping-stones can be adversely affected by the weather. Without a proper base, they can become unstable or settle unevenly. Prepare the base carefully and check the path each spring, adjusting stones as necessary for safety.

TOOLS & MATERIALS

- Basic tools (page 16)
- Sand or compactible gravel
- Stepping stones

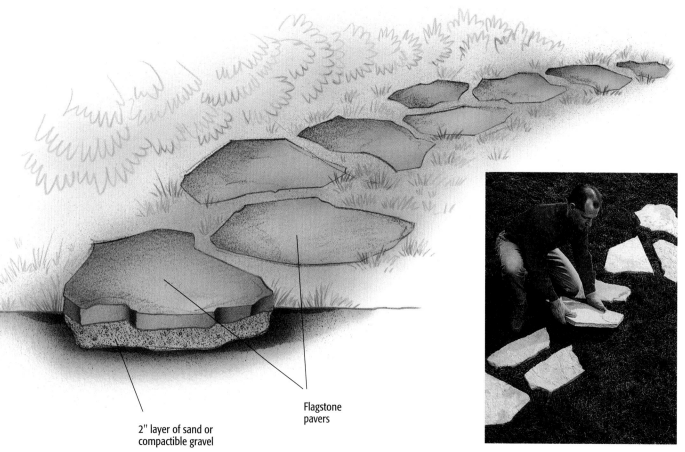

2" layer of sand or compactible gravel

Flagstone pavers

A. *Arrange the stepping stones on top of the grass, then test the layout by walking the path. Adjust the stones as necessary.*

HOW TO CREATE A STEPPING-STONE PATH

Step A: Arrange the Stones

Arrange the stones along the ground in your planned pattern. Walk the full course of the path, then adjust the spacing between the steppers so you can step smoothly from stone to stone.

Step B: Let the Ground Cover Die

If you're installing the path over grass or another living ground cover, leave the stones in place for three to five days. The ground cover beneath the stones will die, leaving a perfect outline of the stones.

Step C: Prepare the Base

1. Using a spade, cut around the outline, creating an excavation 2" deeper than the thickness of the stone.
2. Add a 2" layer of sand or compactible gravel and smooth it out with a garden rake.

Step D: Set & Adjust the Stones

1. Place the stones in the partially filled holes. Rock each stone back and forth several times to help it settle securely into the base.
2. Check to make sure the stones are stable and flush with the ground. Add or remove sand and readjust the stones as necessary.

VARIATION: PLANTING BETWEEN STEPPING-STONES

Consider planting a low-lying, spreading ground cover between the stones for added contrast and texture.

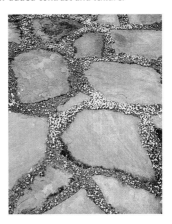

These plants are a few that work well with stepping-stone paths:

- Alyssum
- Rock cress
- Thrift
- Miniature dianthus

- Candytuft
- Lobelia
- Forget-me-not
- Saxifrage
- Sedum

- Thymus
- Scotch moss
- Irish moss
- Woolly thyme
- Mock strawberry

B. *Leave the stones in place for several days to kill the grass beneath, leaving a visible outline for excavation.*

C. *Dig up the outlined areas, 2" deeper than the height of the stones. Spread a 2" layer of sand in each hole.*

D. *Reposition the stones, adding or removing sand as necessary until they're stable and flush with the ground.*

Floors

Flagstone Walkway

Natural flagstone is an ideal material for creating landscape floors. It's attractive and durable, and blends well with both formal and informal landscapes. Although flagstone structures are often mortared, they can also be constructed with the sand-set method. Sand-setting flagstones is much faster and easier than setting them with mortar.

There are a variety of flat, thin sedimentary rocks that can be used for this project. Home and garden stores often carry several types of flagstone, but stone supply yards usually have a greater variety. Some varieties of flagstone cost more than others, but there are many affordable options. When you buy the flagstone for your project, select pieces in a variety of sizes from large to small. Arranging the stones for your walkway is similar to putting together a

puzzle, and you'll need to see all the pieces. When you're ready to begin the project, sort the stones by size, and spread them out so that you can see each one.

The following example demonstrates how to build a straight flagstone walkway with wood edging. If you'd like to build a curved walkway, select another edging material, such as brick or cut stone. Instead of filling gaps between stones with sand, you might want to fill them with topsoil and plant grass or some other ground cover between the stones.

HOW TO BUILD A FLAGSTONE WALKWAY
Step A: Prepare the Site & Install the Edging
1. Lay out, excavate and prepare the base for the walkway (page 72). Remove the stakes and string when the base is complete.
2. Form edging by installing 2 × 6 pressure-treated lumber around the perimeter of the pathway.
3. Drive stakes on the outside of the edging, spaced 12" apart. The tops of the stakes should be below

TOOLS & MATERIALS

- Basic tools (page 16)
- Hand tamp
- Circular saw with masonry blade
- Landscape fabric
- Sand
- 2 × 6 pressure-treated lumber
- Flagstone pavers

Flagstone pavers

Sand

Landscape fabric

Compactible gravel

2 × 6 wood edging

A. *Drive 12" stakes outside the 2 × 6 pressure-treated edging, then attach them together with galvanized screws.*

B. *Test-fit the flagstones inside the edging, mark them for cutting, then set them aside in the same arrangement.*

ground level. Drive galvanized screws through the edging and into the stakes.

Step B: Arrange the Stones

1. Test-fit the stones over the walkway base, finding an attractive arrangement that limits the number of cuts needed. The gaps between the stones should range between ⅜" and 2" wide.

2. Use a pencil to mark the stones for cutting, then remove the stones and place them beside the walkway in the same arrangement.

3. Score along the marked lines with a circular saw and masonry blade set to ⅛" blade depth. Set a piece of wood under the stone, just inside the scored line. Use a masonry chisel and hammer to strike along the scored line until the stone breaks.

Step C: Make a Sand Base

1. Lay strips of landscape fabric over the walkway base, overlapping the strips by 6". (If you plan to grow grass or another ground cover between the stones, skip this step.)

2. Spread a 2" layer of sand over the landscape fabric. Make a "screed" for smoothing the sand from a short 2 × 6, notched to fit inside the edging. (see inset photo) The depth of the notches should equal the thickness of the stones.

3. Pull the screed from one end of the walkway to the other, adding sand as needed to create a level base.

Step D: Lay the Flagstones

1. Beginning at one corner of the walkway, lay the

VARIATION: FLAGSTONE PATIO

Using the same technique for fitting and setting the stones, you can easily create a flagstone patio.

Follow the steps for preparing the patio base, as shown on pages 80 to 81. Then install the wood edging and flagstone as demonstrated below.

flagstones onto the sand base. Repeat the arrangement you created in Step A, with ⅜"- to 2"-wide gaps between stones.

2. If necessary, add or remove sand to level the stones, then set them by tapping them with a rubber mallet or a length of 2 × 4.

Step E: Add Sand Between the Stones

1. Fill the gaps between the stones with sand. (Use topsoil, if you're going to plant grass or ground cover between the stones.)

2. Pack sand into the gaps, then spray the entire walkway with water to help settle the sand.

3. Repeat #2 until the gaps are completely filled and tightly packed with sand.

C. *Spread a 2" layer of sand over the landscape fabric and smooth it out with a screed made from a notched 2 × 6.*

D. *Lay the flagstones in the sand base leaving a gap between stones. Use a rubber mallet to set them in place.*

E. *Pack the gaps between the stones and the edging with sand, then lightly spray the entire walkway with water.*

Floors

Brick Paver Patio

Brick pavers are versatile and durable, making them an excellent material for paving walkways and patios. They convey an impression of formality, quickly dressing up your landscape. Brick pavers are available in a variety of shapes, patterns and colors to complement your landscape. It's best to use concrete pavers rather than traditional clay bricks. Concrete pavers have self-spacing lugs that make them easy to install. To estimate the number of pavers you'll need, see "Estimating Materials" (page 11).

The easiest way to build a patio or walkway with brick pavers is to set them in sand. With this method, the pavers rest on a 1" layer of sand spread over a prepared base. Pavers are then arranged over the sand, and the joints between them are densely packed with more sand. The sand keeps the pavers in place, but still allows them to shift if the ground contracts and expands with temperature changes.

HOW TO BUILD A SAND-SET PAVER PATIO

After you've prepared the foundation for the patio (see "Surface Preparation," page 72), you're ready to begin installing the patio. Leave the stakes and strings in place to use as a reference.

Step A: Prepare the Surface

1. Cut strips of landscape fabric and lay them over the base, overlapping each strip by at least 6".

2. Install rigid plastic edging around the edges of the patio, below the reference strings. Anchor the edging by driving galvanized spikes through the predrilled holes and into the subbase. For curves and rounded patio corners, use rigid plastic edging

TOOLS & MATERIALS

- Basic tools (page 16)
- Hand tamp
- Circular saw with masonry blade
- Landscape fabric
- Sand
- Rigid plastic edging
- 1"-thick pipe
- Brick pavers
- Rented plate compactor
- Broom
- 2 × 4

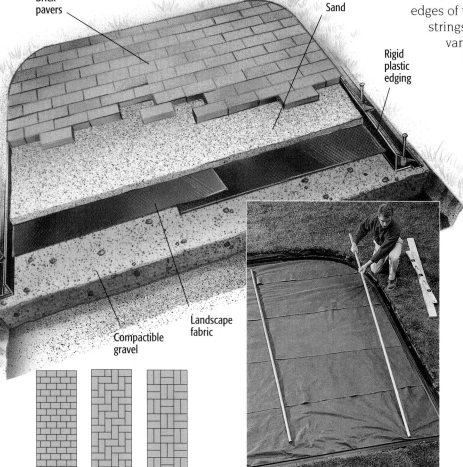

Brick pavers

Sand

Rigid plastic edging

Compactible gravel

Landscape fabric

Staggered   Herringbone   Basket-weave

A. *Cover the excavated area with landscape fabric, install the edging, and space 1" pipes every 6 ft. as spacers.*

B. *Remove the spacers from the 1" layer of sand, fill the depressions with sand and even the sand with a hand tamp.*

with notches on the outside flange.

3. Remove the reference strings, then place 1"-thick pipes or wood strips over the landscape fabric, spaced every 6 ft., to serve as depth spacers for laying the sand base.

Step B: Add the Sand Base

1. Spread a 1" layer of sand over the landscape fabric, using a garden rake to smooth it out. The sand should just cover the tops of the depth spacers.

2. Water the layer of sand thoroughly, then lightly pack it down with a hand tamp.

3. Screed the sand to an even layer by resting a long 2 × 4 on the spacers and drawing it across the sand, using a sawing motion. Fill footprints and low areas with sand, then water, tamp and screed again.

4. Remove the embedded spacers along the sides of the patio base, then fill the grooves with sand and pat them smooth with the hand tamp.

Step C: Set the First Section of Pavers

1. Lay the first border paver in one corner of the patio, making sure it rests firmly against the plastic edging. Lay the next paver snug against the first.

2. Set the pavers by tapping them into the sand with a mallet. Use the depth of the first paver as a guide for setting the remaining pavers in a 2-ft. section.

3. After each section is set, use a long level to make sure the pavers are flat. Make adjustments by tapping high pavers deeper into the sand, or by removing low pavers and adding a thin layer of additional sand underneath them.

Step D: Complete the Patio

1. Continue installing 2-ft.-wide sections of the border and interior pavers.

2. At rounded corners, install border pavers in a fan pattern with even gaps between the pavers. Gentle curves may accommodate full-sized border pavers, but for sharper bends, you'll need to mark and cut wedge-shaped border pavers to fit. Use a circular saw with a masonry blade to cut the pavers.

3. Lay the remaining interior pavers. Use a 2 × 4 to check that the entire patio is level. Adjust any uneven pavers by tapping them with the mallet or by adding more sand beneath them.

Step E: Fill Joints & Compact the Surface

1. Spread a ½" layer of sand over the patio, then use the plate compactor to compress the entire patio and pack the sand into the joints.

2. Sweep up the loose sand, then soak the patio area thoroughly to settle the sand in the joints.

3. Let the surface dry completely. If necessary, spread and pack sand over the patio again, until all the joints are tightly packed.

C. *Lay the pavers tight against each other, setting them with the mallet. Check the height with a level.*

D. *Install border pavers in a fan pattern around the corners, and trim pavers as necessary to make them fit.*

E. *Spread a ½" layer of sand over the patio and pack it into the joints with the plate compactor. Sweep up the loose sand.*

Concrete Patio

Concrete is an inexpensive material for creating durable, low-maintenance outdoor floors. It can be formed into almost any shape or size, making it an ideal choice for walkways, driveways and patios.

The patio in our project is divided into four even quadrants separated by permanent forms. This construction method makes it possible to complete the project in four easy stages—you can pour, tool and seed each quadrant separately.

An isolation joint separates the patio from the foundation of the house, so footings aren't necessary. When calculating the depth of the base, remember to maintain adequate clearance between the top of the patio and the door threshold. The top of the patio should be at least 2" below the house sill or threshold, so the concrete has room to rise and fall without suffering damage from frost heave.

Concrete may be left as is or finished with a variety of techniques to give the surface an attractive texture or pattern. For this project, we added color and texture with a layer of seeding aggregate.

TOOLS & MATERIALS

- Basic tools (page 16)
- Masonry hoe
- Wood float
- Concrete edger
- Stiff-bristled brush
- Paint roller

- Pressure-treated 2 × 4s
- Stakes
- String
- 2½" deck screws
- Masking tape

- Wire mesh
- Bolsters
- Concrete mix
- Plastic
- Seeding aggregate
- Exposed aggregate sealer

HOW TO CONSTRUCT A CONCRETE PATIO

Step A: Prepare the Surface & Build the Forms

1. Lay out the patio, excavate the site and prepare the base (page 72). Leave the stakes and string in place as a reference.
2. Measure and cut pressure-treated 2 × 4s for the permanent form outlining the entire patio.
3. Lay the boards in place, using the strings as guides. Fasten the ends with 2½" deck screws.
4. Temporarily stake the forms at 2-ft. intervals, then use a 2 × 4 and a level to make sure the frame is level.

Step B: Divide the Form into Quadrants

1. Measure, mark and cut the 2 × 4s that divide the patio into quadrants. Attach these pieces to the frame with toenailed deck screws.
2. Drive deck screws halfway into the inside faces of

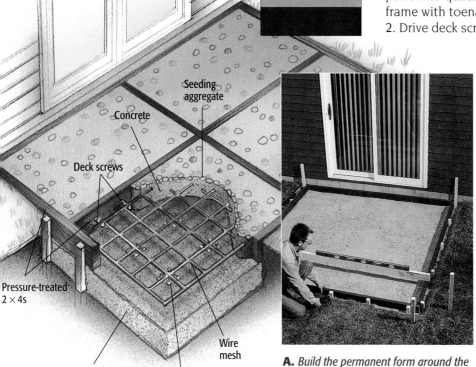

Seeding aggregate

Concrete

Deck screws

Pressure-treated 2 × 4s

Compactible gravel

Bolster

Wire mesh

Cement

Bolster

Wire mesh

A. *Build the permanent form around the patio perimeter and temporarily stake it into place, using a level as you work.*

B. *Install the 2 × 4s that divide the patio into four quadrants and attach them to the frame with deck screws.*

all the forms, spacing them every 12". These exposed screws will act as tie rods between the poured concrete and the forms.

3. Cover the tops of the forms with masking tape to protect them when you pour the concrete.

Step C: Pour the Concrete for the First Quadrant

1. Cut reinforcing wire mesh to fit inside each quadrant, leaving 1" clearance on all sides. Use bolsters to raise the mesh off the base, making sure it remains at least 2" below the top of the forms.

2. Mix the concrete in a wheelbarrow, then pour it into the first quadrant. Use a masonry hoe to spread the concrete evenly in the form.

3. Screed the concrete with a straight 2 × 4 that is long enough to reach across a quadrant.

4. Slide a spade along the inside edges of the form, then rap the outer edges with a hammer to settle the concrete into the quadrant.

Step D: Embed the Aggregate

1. Sprinkle handfuls of seeding aggregate evenly over the wet concrete.

2. Use a float to embed the aggregate. Make sure that the aggregate is firmly embedded, but still visible.

3. Tool the edges of the quadrant with a concrete edger, then use a wood float to smooth out any marks left by the tool. Cover the seeded concrete with plastic so it doesn't cure too quickly as you pour and finish the remaining quadrants.

4. Pour concrete into and finish the remaining quad-

VARIATION: WALKWAY

Using the same technique as used to finish the patio's surface, you can give a freshly poured concrete walkway an exposed aggregate finish. Apply the finish a section at a time for best results.

rants, one at a time, using the same technique.

Step E: Complete the Finish & Seal the Concrete

1. After the water has evaporated from the concrete surface, mist it with water, then scrub it with a stiff-bristled brush to expose the aggregate.

2. Remove the tape from the forms, then replace the plastic and let the concrete cure for one week. After the concrete has cured, rinse and scrub the aggregate again to remove any remaining residue.

3. Wait three weeks, then seal the patio surface with exposed-aggregate sealer. Apply the sealer according to the manufacturer's directions.

C. *Pour concrete into the first quadrant and screed the concrete smooth with a 2 × 4 that rests on top of the form.*

D. *Sprinkle handfuls of seeding aggregate evenly over the surface of the wet concrete and embed it with a float.*

E. *Mist the surface of the concrete with water and scrub it with a stiff-bristled brush to expose the aggregate.*

Floors

Platform Deck

A freestanding platform deck is a low-maintenance option for creating an outdoor floor. Because it can be constructed virtually anywhere, in almost any size, a platform deck works in nearly any landscape. The wood can be left natural, stained or painted to blend with your house and other landscape elements.

A deck built from weather-resistant materials will last for years. Galvanized hardware, which resists rust and corrosion, helps a deck remain strong and stable.

You'll be able to build this deck over a single weekend. It uses lumber in standard lengths, so you won't need to do a lot of cutting. In addition, this deck uses precast concrete footings, rather than poured footings. These precast footings are available at home improvement centers and lumberyards.

Our 12 × 12-ft. deck rests on a 10 × 10-ft. base formed by 18 concrete footings arranged in three rows of six footings each. Joists are secured in slots in the tops of the footings, simplifying the building process. If you're building your deck on sloped or uneven ground, you'll need to use 4 × 4 posts that fit in the center of the footings to level the joists (see page 86 for further information).

TOOLS & MATERIALS

- Basic tools (page 16)
- Paintbrush
- Circular saw
- Framing square
- Wood stakes
- Precast concrete footings (18)
- 12-ft. 2 × 6s (38)
- Wood sealer/protectant
- 2 lbs. galvanized 3" deck screws

HOW TO BUILD A PLATFORM DECK

Step A: Install & Level the Footings

1. Measure a 10 × 10-ft. area for the deck foundation, and mark the corners with stakes.
2. Position a footing at each corner, then measure from corner to corner, from the center of each footing. Adjust until the diagonal measurements are equal, which means the footings are square.
3. Place a 2 × 6 across the corner footings

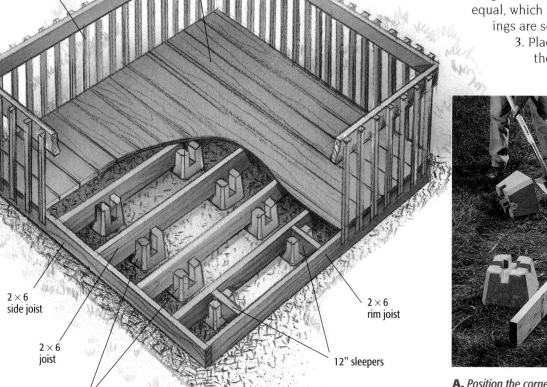

2 × 6 hand rail

2 × 6 decking spaced ⅛" apart

2 × 2s spaced 4" apart

2 × 6 side joist

2 × 6 joist

Precast concrete footings

12" sleepers

2 × 6 rim joist

A. *Position the corner footings and the center footing for the back joist. Remove or add soil beneath the footings to level them.*

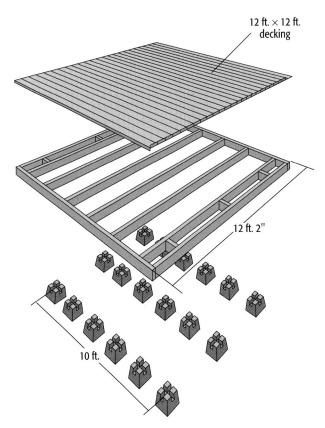

12 ft. × 12 ft. decking

12 ft. 2"

10 ft.

for the back row, setting it in the center slots. Check this joist with a level, then add or remove soil beneath footings as necessary to level it.

4. Center a footing between these corner footings. Use a level to recheck the joist, then add or remove soil beneath the center footing, if necessary. Remove the joist.

5. Repeat the process described in #3, #4 and #5 to set and level the footings for the front row.

6. Position the remaining 12 footings at equal intervals, aligned in three rows. Position a 2 × 6 from the front row of footings to the back, and adjust soil as necessary to bring the interior footings into alignment with, the front and back rows.

Step B: Install the Joists

1. Seal the ends of each 2 × 6 with wood sealer/protectant and let them dry completely.

2. Center a 12-ft. joist across each row of footings. Using a level, check the joists once again and carefully adjust the footings if necessary.

Step C: Add the Side Joists & Rim Joists

1. Line up a 2 × 6 flush against the ends of the joists along the left side of the deck, with the ends extending equally past the front and back joists.

2. Attach the side joist by driving a pair of deck screws into each joist.

3. Repeat this process to install the right side joist.

4. At the front of the deck, position a 2 × 6 rim joist flush between the ends of the side joists, forming a

butt joint on each end.

5. Attach the rim joist to the side joists by driving a pair of deck screws through the faces of the side joists, into the ends of the rim joist.

6. Repeat #1 and #2 to install the other rim joist.

Step D: Position the Sleepers

1. Measure and cut six 2 × 6 sleepers to fit between the front and back joists and the rim joists. Seal the cut ends with wood sealer/protectant and let them

B. *Position the remaining footings and insert the joists. Check to make sure the framework is level, and adjust as needed.*

C. *Install the front and back rim joists between the ends of the side joists, securing them with pairs of deck screws.*

D. *Position the sleepers in the slots of the footings, then attach them to the joists on both sides with pairs of deck screws.*

Platform Deck (cont.)

E. *After the framing is completed, measure the diagonals and adjust the frame until it's square.*

F. *Install the decking by driving a pair of screws into each joist. Use a framing square to leave a ⅛" space between boards.*

dry completely.

2. Position one sleeper in each row of footings, between the first joist and the rim joist. Attach each sleeper by driving a pair of galvanized deck screws through each of the joists and into the sleeper.

Step E: Square Up the Frame

1. Once the framing is complete, measure the diagonals from corner to corner. Compare the measurements to see if they are equal.

2. Adjust the framing as necessary by pushing it into alignment. You'll need a helper to hold one side of

the framework while you push against the other.

Step F: Install the Decking

1. Seal the 2 × 6 decking boards with wood sealer/ protectant and let them dry. Seal all exposed framing members as well.

2. Lay a 2 × 6 over the surface of the deck, perpendicular to the joists and flush with the rim joist. Secure this board with deck screws.

3. Repeat # 2 to install the rest of the decking. Use a framing square to set a ⅛" space between boards. You may need to rip cut the last decking board.

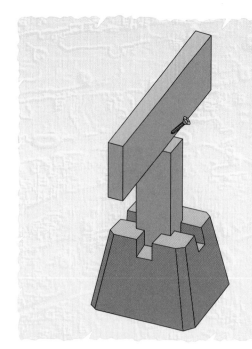

TIP: LEVELING WITH POSTS

If you're building your deck on sloped or uneven ground, you'll need to use 4 × 4 posts that fit in the center of the footings to level the joists.

Measure the distance between the bottom of the leveled joist and the square depression in the center of the footing. Measure, mark and cut a 4 × 4 post to this length. Place the post in the footing, then secure it by driving deck screws at an angle through the bottom of the joist into the post.

VARIATION: ADDING A RAILING

TOOLS & MATERIALS

- 12-ft. 2 × 6s (3)
- 42" 2 × 2s (one end beveled)
- Drill
- Level
- 2½" galvanized deck screws

Although this platform deck rests low to the ground, you may want to add a hand rail around two or three sides of the deck, especially if the deck will be used by young children or an elderly person. For each side of the deck to which you're adding railings, you'll need 25 2 × 2s, 42" long.

Step A:

1. Place the 2 × 2s flush together, adjust them so the ends are even, and draw a pair of straight lines, 3" apart, across each board, 1½" above the beveled end. Repeat the process and draw a single line 2¾" from the top of the other end. Using the lines as guides, drill pilot holes into the 2 × 2s.

2. Apply wood sealer/protectant to the ends of the 2 × 2s.

Step B:

1. Position a 2 × 2 flush with the bottom of the joist, then clamp it in place to use as a placement guide.

2. Position the corner 2 × 2s against the side joists, beveled end down, 4" in from the corner. Check for plumb, then drive deck screws through the pilot holes.

3. Attach the remaining 2 × 2s for each side, spacing them 4" apart.

Step C:

1. Hold a 12-ft. 2 × 6 that forms the top of the railing in place, behind the installed 2 × 2s.

2. Attach the 2 × 2s to the 2 × 6 top rails by driving deck screws through the pilot holes.

3. Connect the top rails at the corners, using pairs of deck screws.

4. Finish the railing by applying a coat of wood sealer, according to the manufacturer's directions.

A. Gang together the 2 × 2s, then drill a pair of pilot holes into the beveled ends, and a single pilot hole in the opposite end.

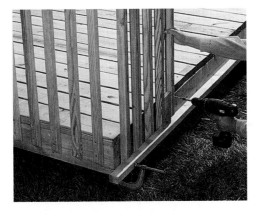

B. Attach the 2 × 2s to the side joists, leaving a 4" gap between them.

C. Level the 2 × 6 railing behind the 2 × 2s, then attach it by driving screws through the pilot holes.

Soil Preparation

Soil preparation is the most important step in establishing new lawns and other living ground covers. When you're starting from scratch, good soil preparation ensures that your lawn has the foundation it needs to develop a strong, healthy root system. Whether you're using grass seed, sod or planting another ground cover, the process of preparing the soil remains the same.

SIZING UP YOUR SOIL

The first step in soil preparation is finding out the condition of your existing soil. Start by getting a test done on the soil in the area where you plan to establish a lawn. For more information on collecting soil samples and getting a soil test report, see "Soil" (page 14). The soil test report will include information on the type of soil you have, the nutrient levels present and whether or not the soil is capable of supporting a healthy lawn. If the soil is within a desirable range, the report will also include detailed instructions for amending and fertilizing it.

AMENDING THE SOIL

If the test report indicates that you merely need to amend the soil, purchase the recommended amendments and rent a tiller to blend them into the soil.

Following manufacturer's instructions, set the tiller so that it digs to a depth between 4" and 6" (see photo, opposite page). Spread an even layer of the amendments over the surface of a small area and till them into the soil. Work your way across the yard in the same pattern you would use for mowing the grass. Once the entire lawn area is tilled, regrade and level the soil as necessary.

BRINGING IN NEW SOIL

If your soil fails the lawn compatibility test, don't despair. You can purchase high quality topsoil to add to your existing soil. Topsoil, also called "black dirt," is sold by

Preparing the soil properly is one of the most important steps in establishing a thick, healthy lawn.

the cubic yard and can be delivered by soil contractors (below).

It's important not to create two distinct layers of soil, so you need to prepare the existing soil to mix with the new topsoil. Dig several small holes, then inspect and feel the texture of the existing soil. If it isn't severely compacted, you can simply loosen it with a tiller before adding topsoil. If, on the other hand, the existing soil is heavily compacted, hire a contractor to "slice" it before you add the topsoil. Slicing is performed by heavy machinery outfitted with a blade. The blade makes deep cuts into the soil, loosening it up and eliminating compaction.

When you order topsoil, give the contractor the dimensions of your lawn and order enough topsoil to spread a 4" layer over the entire area. If you're covering a large area, you may want to hire the contractor to distribute the soil as well as deliver it.

Even if the area you're covering seems manageable, consider asking friends or hiring someone to help you spread the soil. It's not difficult, but it takes some time and effort. Drop wheelbarrow loads of soil around the area, then use a rake to distribute the soil evenly over the entire surface. When all the soil is distributed, check and correct the grade of the yard (page 24).

SMOOTHING THE SURFACE

To create a smooth, even surface for seeding, sodding or planting ground cover, you'll need to slightly compress the soil. The goal is to lightly smooth the surface without compacting the soil. Fill a landscape drum ⅓ full with water, then roll it over the surface, walking in a row-by-row pattern (photo, right).

To amend the soil, begin by spreading an even layer of the prescribed amendments over the area. Then use a tiller to blend the amendments into the soil, working in a small area at a time.

(above) Order enough topsoil to spread a 4" to 6" layer over your existing soil. Before you spread new topsoil, loosen existing soil with a tiller or hire a contractor to "slice" the soil.

(left) Lightly compact the soil with a landscape drum. Roll it over the lawn, walking in a row-by-row pattern.

Seed Lawn

Seeding is the easiest and least expensive way to start a new lawn. But, there are a couple of factors you'll need to consider: The time of year, the type of grass seed used, the condition of the soil and the amount of water the seed receives all contribute to the success of a seeded lawn.

Timing is essential when seeding a new lawn. The best time to seed is during the growing season for grass shoots—the parts of a grass plant that spread and grow new leaves, forming a dense lawn. The timing of this window of opportunity varies, depending on where you live. In warmer climates, shoot growth primarily occurs in the spring. In cooler climates, there are two shoot-growth seasons—one in the

early spring, and another in the early fall. Many experts feel that fall is the ideal time to seed lawns in colder climates, because fewer weeds are present and more frequent rains and cooler temperatures keep the grass seed moist.

When buying grass seed, choose a variety that's suited to your climate.(For more information on selecting seed, see the tip on page 93.) Grass seed is commonly sold in blends combining several different varieties of grasses. Purchase grass seed with a low percentage of crop, inert matter and weeds, and a high germination percentage for each of the desired grasses.

Soil condition is another factor that determines the success of seeding a lawn. The ideal soil for seeding has been properly prepared, as shown in "Soil Preparation" (page 88), and moistened to a depth of 4" to 6". Moisture not only nourishes the seeds, it protects them—seeds tend to blow away if the soil is too dry. Although the soil needs to be moist, try to avoid seeding just before a heavy rainfall, which could wash seeds away.

Once you've seeded a lawn, keep the soil moist during the germination period, a minimum of two weeks. After the germination period, water the grass as needed, making sure it receives a total of about 1" to 1½" of water a week in rainfall plus irrigation. If puddles

TOOLS & MATERIALS

- Broadcast spreader
- Leaf rake
- Landscape drum
- Grass seed

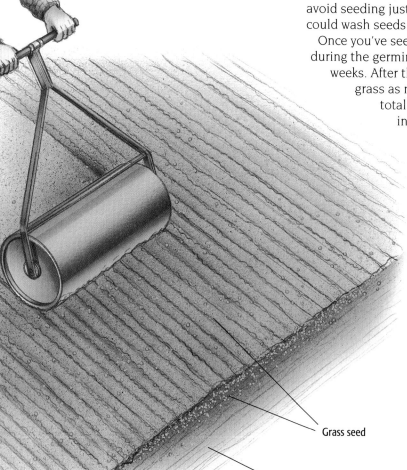

Grass seed

4" to 6" layer of topsoil

A. *Fill the broadcast spreader with grass seed in the amount listed on the package.*

form, stop watering until they recede. Don't overwater your new lawn—too much water encourages fungal problems and root disease.

HOW TO SEED A NEW LAWN

Step A: Prepare the Soil

1. Prepare the soil as shown on page 88. Water the soil until it's moist to a depth of 4" to 6".
2. Place a broadcast spreader on a paved surface, such as a driveway. Fill the spreader with the amount of grass recommended on the seed package.

Step B: Spread the Seed

1. Establish the desired rate of seed coverage by calibrating the spreader according to the recommendations on the seed package.
2. Apply the seed in two stages, following a grid pattern to ensure even coverage. First, push the spreader back and forth across the yard in straight passes. When you've covered the entire area, push the spreader up and down the yard, perpendicular to the first application.

Step C: Cover & Water the Seed

1. Use a rake to lightly rake the soil until only 10% to 15% of the seed is visible.
2. Lightly compact the raked soil by rolling over it with a half-filled landscape drum.
3. Water the yard until the soil is moist to a depth of 6", then keep the seed moist for several weeks.

TIP: READING GRASS SEED LABELS:

The type of grass you select will play a large part in the success of your lawn. But it can be difficult to tell exactly what you're buying. Whether it's a prepackaged blend or seed sold by the pound in bulk, there will always be a label that tells you exactly what type of seeds are included in that blend.

Lush Lawn Blend

Grass Seed & Supply Co., Fairtown, MN

Lot. No.: 5546-89   Test Date: 06/06/98

Pure Seed	Variety	Germination
42%	Colonel Kentucky Bluegrass	88%
33%	Fine Perennial Ryegrass	78%
21%	Red Tall Fescue	80%
0.4%	Inert Matter	
1.2%	Crop	
2.4%	Weed	

Pure Seed: the percentage of seeds for each variety that are capable of growing.

Germination: the portion of the pure seed that will germinate within a reasonable amount of time.

Inert Matter: materials present in the blend, such as broken seeds, hulls and chaff, that aren't capable of growing.

Crop: the percentage of agricultural grain and undesirable grass seed contained in the blend.

Weed: the portion of weed seeds present in the blend.

B. *Calibrate the spreader according to the seed package's instructions, then push the spreader across the lawn in two passes, following a grid pattern for even coverage.*

C. *Lightly rake the seed into the soil, then roll a landscape drum over the soil.*

Sod Lawn

Installing sod is the quickest way to create a new lawn. Within a few hours, you can transform bare dirt into a lushly carpeted lawn. It's simple to create a beautiful lawn from sod, but it does require a little planning, thorough preparation and some heavy work. To succeed, you need properly prepared soil, quality sod, careful installation and adequate water.

Sod can be installed at any time from the beginning of the spring through early fall, but it's best to avoid installing it during especially hot, dry weather. You can purchase sod from a sod farm, landscape supply store or landscape contractor. When you compare prices, make sure all the quotes include delivery; most suppliers charge a fee for delivering small orders. For the best results, request that your sod be cut within 24 hours of delivery. After the sod arrives, store it in a shaded area, and install it within one day of delivery. Keep the sod moist, but don't soak it. Sod that drys out won't establish roots, but overwatered sod is heavy and difficult to install.

Good soil preparation is vital: the soil should be properly amended, smooth and free from rocks or construction debris. Sod roots need to have contact with moist soil. If your soil is dry, water it the night before you plan to lay the sod.

Once the sod is laid, keep it constantly moist for three days. Following this period, water your lawn as often as needed to keep the first 4" of soil moist, as described on page 90. During extended hot, dry weather, you'll need to water the sod frequently.

HOW TO INSTALL SOD
Step A: Establish a Pattern
1. Following the guidelines on pages 88 to 89, prepare the soil.
2. Select a straight border, such as a walkway to use as a reference guide. If there isn't a straight surface in the immediate area, sprinkle flour on the ground

TOOLS & MATERIALS

- Basic tools (page 16)
- Sod knife
- Landscape drum
- Fresh sod
- Flour
- Topsoil
- Stakes

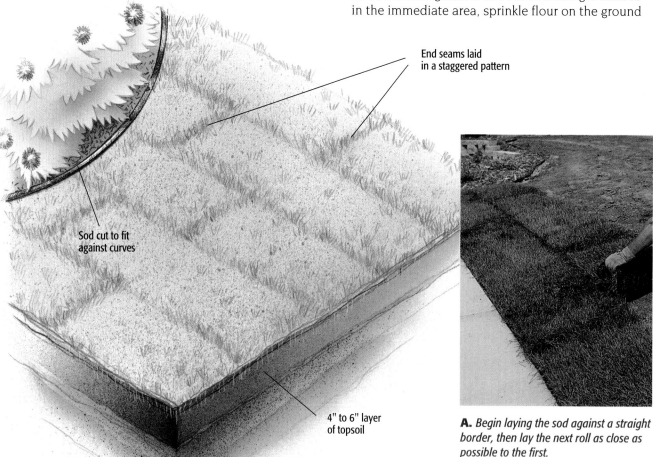

End seams laid in a staggered pattern

Sod cut to fit against curves

4" to 6" layer of topsoil

A. *Begin laying the sod against a straight border, then lay the next roll as close as possible to the first.*

as a reference line. Working parallel to your reference guide, install the first roll of sod. Firmly push the sod into the soil.

3. Continue placing rolls parallel to the guide, butting the seams as closely as possible. To help eliminate the appearance of seams, stagger the end seams.

Step B: Camouflage the Seams

1. Lift the edges of pieces that butt against each other, then press the edges down, knitting the two pieces together.

2. As each new piece is laid, cover the seams with ½" of topsoil to prevent the edges from drying out.

Step C: Stake the Slopes & Trim the Edges

1. Continue laying the sod, staggering the end seams. When sodding a slope, drive wooden stakes through the sod, 4" to 6" into the soil, to hold the sod in place.

2. Use a sod knife to trim excess sod around walkway curves, planting beds and trees.

Step D: Roll the Sod

1. Roll over the sod with a half-filled landscape drum, pressing the sod firmly into the soil.

2. Water the sod until it's thoroughly saturated.

TIP: GRASS SEED OR SOD— WHAT CHOICE IS BEST FOR YOU?

If you're starting a new lawn, you'll want to choose the method that works best for your situation. Seeding and sodding each have benefits, as well as drawbacks. Time, money, climate, maintenance requirements and the amount of stress the lawn will endure are all factors to take into account as you choose the best method for establishing a new lawn.

Sod	Seed
• Expensive	• Inexpensive
• Immediate results	• Takes longer to develop
• Limited variety of grasses	• Wide variety of grasses
• Establishes well on slopes	• Establishes strong root systems
• Fewer weeds	• Ideal planting times limited
• Heavy work	• Daily watering

B. Lift up the edges of adjoining sod pieces, then press them down together, blending the seam between the pieces.

C. Use stakes to secure sod installed on sloped areas, then trim excess sod around curves with a sod cutter.

D. After installing all of the sod, use a half-filled landscape drum to seat it firmly.

Lawn Renovation

Renovation can significantly improve the appearance of an established lawn. The process involves diagnosing and remedying lawn problems, then topseeding and fertilizing the lawn to grow a new crop of healthy grass. Typical conditions corrected during renovation include an abundance of weeds, large bare areas, excessive thatch buildup and soil compaction.

Before you begin planning your renovation, get your soil tested. For detailed information on requesting a soil report, see "Soil" (page 14). The soil test report will be available three to six weeks after you submit soil samples. This report will include detailed information on soil content and how it should be amended to support a healthy lawn.

Next, you need to determine what weeds currently are present in your lawn and evaluate the balance between weeds and grass. If you find weeds that you can't identify, take samples to a local nursery or extension service for more information. If over 40% of

your lawn consists of weeds, simple renovation won't solve the problem—experts recommend demolishing the lawn and starting over again from scratch.

As a final step in the evaluation process, cut a small, 6"-deep pie-shaped wedge out of your lawn. Using this sample, measure the level of thatch, the layer of partially decomposed pieces of grass sitting on top of the soil (below, left). Healthy lawns include a moderate layer of thatch, but heavy layers can cause problems. If the thatch is more than $\frac{1}{2}$" thick, add thatch removal to your renovation plan.

Finally, check the moisture content of the soil in the wedge. If the soil isn't moist all the way to the bottom, you need to add water. The soil should be moist to a depth of 6" before you begin work. Depending on the current conditions, it could take several days for the soil to reach adequate moisture levels, so plan accordingly.

HOW TO RENOVATE A LAWN
Step A: Eliminate the Weeds
Spot-kill the weeds in your lawn by applying weed killer, using a pressure sprayer. Wear gloves, safety goggles, a particle mask and protective clothing when using weed killer. Use a broadleaf herbicide to kill broadleaf weeds, such as dandelion and clover. For grassy weeds, such as crabgrass and quackgrass, use a nonselective herbicide containing glyphosate.

TOOLS & MATERIALS

- Basic tools (page 16)
- Pressure sprayer
- Vertical mower
- Leaf rake
- Aerator
- Broadcast spreader
- Gloves
- Goggles
- Particle mask
- Soil test report
- Fertilizer
- Grass seed

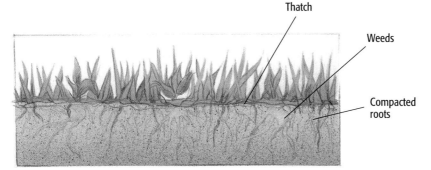

Thatch

Weeds

Compacted roots

Aerated soil

Grass seed

A. *Wearing protective clothing and gear, apply weed killer to the affected areas.*

Glyphosate kills all grass, plants, shrubs or trees it comes into contact with, so apply it carefully, and plan to replant affected areas, as shown in "Seed Lawn" (page 90), and "Sod Lawn" (pages 92).

Step B: Remove Thatch Buildup

1. Remove thatch with a rented vertical mower, also called a power rake. Set the tines on the vertical mower to rake about ¼" below the surface of the soil.
2. Push the vertical mower over the entire lawn in a series of straight passes, then go over it again in perpendicular rows, covering the area in a grid pattern.
3. Rake up and discard the removed thatch.

Step C: Loosen the Soil

1. Relieve soil compaction and improve drainage by removing small cores of soil from your lawn with a rented aerator. Run the machine across the lawn, using the same grid pattern described in Step B.
2. Let the soil cores partially dry, then rake them up.
3. Using the vertical mower or a leaf rake, scratch the entire surface of the lawn to loosen the soil slightly.

Step D: Fertilize & Topseed the Lawn

1. Fill a broadcast spreader with the fertilizer blend recommended in the soil test report.
2. Calibrate the spreader according to the directions on the fertilizer package. Distribute the fertilizer, covering the lawn in perpendicular rows.
3. Fill the spreader with grass seed. Topseed the entire lawn (page 91).

TIP: REPAIRING BARE SPOTS

It's an all-too-familiar sight—an otherwise attractive lawn marred by bare spots. If your lawn is plagued with dying areas, you'll need to determine the cause and take preventive measures to keep the grass from dying again. Once the problem is solved, sprinkle grass seed over the bare area, lightly rake it into the soil, and gently tamp the soil down. Keep the area moist for at least two weeks while the seed germinates. Use the following guidelines to resolve common problems:

Cause	Solution
Dog damage	Immediately water areas where the dog urinates.
Compacted soil	Aerate the area, or till in an amendment, such as compost or peat moss.
Chemical burn	Remove several inches of topsoil from the bare area.
Disease	Consult your local extension service for diagnosis and treatment.
Foot traffic	Install a path or stepping stones to accommodate traffic.
Insects	Consult your local extension service for recommendations.

B. *Use a vertical mower to remove significant thatch buildup from the lawn.*

C. *Improve the lawn's soil structure by removing cores of soil with an aerator.*

D. *Apply the prescribed fertilizer blend to the lawn with a broadcast spreader.*

Accents

Once your outdoor rooms are constructed, your landscape is like an empty house; it needs to be furnished and decorated to become a real home. Whether they're functional or purely decorative, accents give your landscape its personality and complete its transformation from a traditional yard into a series of outdoor living spaces.

Seating is an essential element for a comfortable outdoor home. In fact, placing a wood bench next to a tree can be enough to form a special room for quiet contemplation. With a little spare time and a few basic household tools, you can build a wood bench that would complement almost any outdoor room.

Traditional garden beds serve many purposes: hiding the foundation of the house, adding color and year-round interest, growing vegetables and herbs for cooking or showcasing a prized collection of roses. If your soil is poor, a raised garden bed may be a more hospitable home for your favorite plants and flowers. And whether your yard is large or small, container gardens add splashes of color to pathways, patios and fences without taking up much space.

One of the most appealing accents you can build is a garden pond. These decorative ponds introduce new colors, textures and sounds into the landscape, creating a soothing place to relax and observe nature. Using a ready-made pond liner, you can create a water garden to showcase aquatic plants, brightly colored fish or even a fountain.

Accessorizing your landscape is often the most enjoyable part of the landscaping process. However, be careful not to get carried away—too many accents can make a landscape feel cluttered or crowded. Instead, strive to keep a balance between landscape elements and accents. Whenever possible, repeat colors, plants and materials found elsewhere in your yard. Using this technique, you'll create an attractive, visually unified outdoor home.

IN THIS CHAPTER:

Accents

Bench

A garden bench makes a decorative and functional addition to almost any area in your yard. Wood garden benches are especially charming; the color and texture of the wood blends in with both formal and informal landscapes. Many garden centers and mail-order catalogs sell beautiful wood garden benches, but you can easily build an attractive, high-quality bench yourself at a fraction of the cost.

Our bench is 5 ft. long, and can seat several adults comfortably. The basic framework is made up of leg pairs joined by aprons. The seat, which is formed by two planks, fits flush into the top of the frame and is attached to the aprons.

Because the bench will be exposed to the elements, use galvanized hardware and moisture-resistant wood glue. Sealing the cut ends with a wood sealer/preservative will also increase the life span of your bench.

HOW TO BUILD A CEDAR BENCH

Step A: Build the Legs & Attach the Aprons

1. Cut eight 17"-long leg pieces from 1 × 4 cedar, using a circular saw. To form each leg, apply a bead of glue to the long edge of one board. Butt the long edge of the glued board flush against the face of another board, forming an L-shaped leg. Drill five evenly spaced, counterbored ⅜" pilot holes into the side of the butt joint. Sink 2" deck screws through the pilot holes. Following the same process, assemble the remaining three legs.

2. Cut two 18½" short aprons from 2 × 4 lumber. Position an apron flush against the inside faces of two legs, adjusting until the top of the apron is 1½" down from the tops of the legs.

3. Glue the apron to the legs. Drill a pair of pilot holes in the ends of the apron. Drive 2" deck screws through the pilot holes and into the legs. Using the same technique, attach the other apron to the remaining legs.

Step B: Attach the Long Aprons

1. Cut two 57"-long aprons from 1 × 4

TOOLS & MATERIALS

- Basic tools (page 16)
- Circular saw
- ⅜" counterbore bit
- Bar clamp
- Palm sander
- 8-ft. 1 × 4s (3)
- 6-ft. 2 × 10s (2)
- 8-ft. 2 × 4 (1)
- Wood glue
- Wood sealer /protectant
- 1½", 2" deck screws
- ⅜" cedar plugs

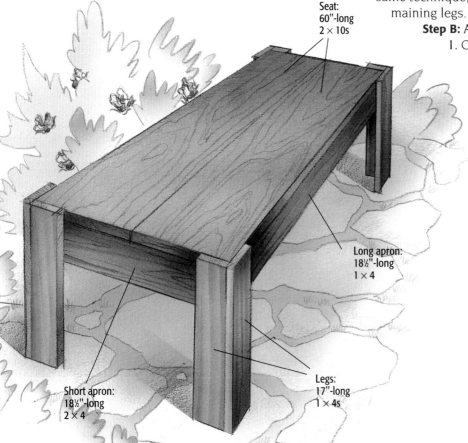

Seat: 60"-long 2 × 10s

Long apron: 18½"-long 1 × 4

Short apron: 18½"-long 2 × 4

Legs: 17"-long 1 × 4s

A. Assemble the legs. Attach the short aprons , 1½" down from the tops of the legs, using wood glue and 2" deck screws.

98

lumber. Apply glue to the ends of one apron and position it against the inside of the leg assemblies, flush with the tops of the short aprons. Drill a pair of counterbored pilot holes, then attach the leg assemblies to the aprons with 1½" deck screws.

2. Flip the frame over and use the same process to install the other long apron to the leg assembly.

Step C: Make the Seat & Fasten the Cleats

1. Cut two 60"-long seat slats from 2 × 10 lumber, and three 16¾"-long cleats from 2 × 4 lumber. Clamp the seat slats together, edge to edge, with a bar clamp, making sure that the ends are flush.

2. Use glue and 2" screws to secure the cleats to the slats. The end cleats should be inset 1½" from the end and ¾" from the edges.

Step D: Attach the Seat & Finish the Wood

1. Attach the seat to the leg assembly with glue and 2" deck screws driven through the aprons and into the seat cleats. Make sure to drill counterbored pilot holes for the screws.

2. Glue ⅜"-diameter cedar wood plugs into all the counterbores. Let the glue dry, then use a palm sander to sand the plugs until they're flush with the face of the wood.

3. Finish-sand the exposed wood surfaces with a palm sander. Wipe the bench clean and apply an even coat of exterior wood stain.

VARIATION: STONE SLAB BENCH

You can build an attractive stone bench using only three stones. The bench is constructed by placing the seat slab on top of the two smaller support stones that act as legs.

Although the bench is easy to build, you'll need stones of a specific shape. For the seat, you'll need a large, flat stone. For the legs, you'll need two stones about the same length, with one flat end. Stone quarries and aggregate centers usually carry stones this size and will deliver them for a fee.

Space the support stones 24" to 36" apart, and set them in trenches 6" deep. Center the seat slab on top of the support stones. If the top wobbles, wedge a small, flat stone between the seat and the support stones.

B. *Position the long aprons against the insides of the legs, flush against the short aprons. Secure them in place with glue and 2" deck screws.*

C. *Make the seat from a pair of 2 × 10s. Glue a cleat 1½" from each end, then center a third cleat between them. Fasten the cleats with 2" deck screws.*

D. *Set the seat into the frame. Drill pilot holes through the aprons into the cleats. Secure the seat in place with deck screws.*

Accents

Garden Bed

Garden beds give your yard a finished look by adding color, shape and texture to the landscape. They also help define boundaries between outdoor rooms and soften transitions between architectural structures and the yard. Garden beds can be added almost anywhere, in both sunny and shady areas.

Mixing perennials and annuals is a popular choice for sunny or shady garden beds. Another option is to plant garden beds for year-round seasonal interest, using a combination of bulbs, shrubs, annuals and perennials. Many people also devote garden beds to growing vegetables and herbs.

Although you can create a garden bed in any shape, professional landscape designers recommend creating beds with curves. Curved beds are more visually appealing than straight ones and add variety to your landscape.

Before you create a planting bed, have a soil test conducted on the soil in the proposed location. Give the soil testing lab a list of the types of plants you plan to grow; the soil test report will include detailed instructions for amending your soil to support these plants. If your soil cannot be amended to support your garden, the best alternative is to build a raised bed (page 102).

HOW TO MAKE A GARDEN BED

Step A: Outline & Clear the Site

1. Using a rope or garden hose, outline the shape of the garden bed on the site you've chosen.
2. Remove all of the grass and other plants inside the outlined area with a garden spade. If the area has a lot of weeds, you might want to use a nonselective herbicide first, which will kill everything growing inside the outline.

Step B: Prepare the Bed

1. Apply an even layer of the recommended amendments and fertilizers over the soil.
2. Mix the amendments into the soil with a shovel or rented tiller. For flower beds, blend amendments to a depth of 6". For vegetable beds, till to a depth of 10".

TOOLS & MATERIALS

- Basic tools (page 16)
- Motorized tiller
- Rope or garden hose
- Soil test report
- Soil amendments
- Flexible plastic edging
- Plants
- Mulch

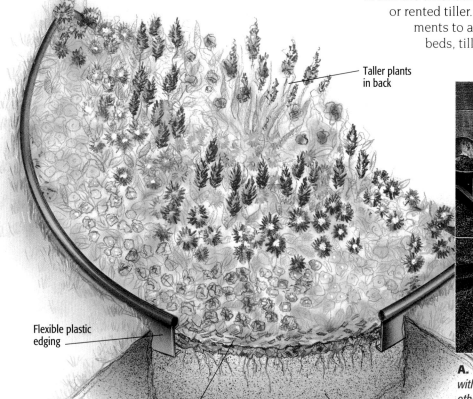

Taller plants in back

Flexible plastic edging

2" to 3" layer of mulch

6" to 10" layer of tilled, amended soil

A. *Outline the shape of the garden bed with a hose, then remove any grass or other plants growing inside the outline.*

3. Dig a narrow edging trench along the perimeter of the bed. Make the depth of the trench equal to the height of the edging.

4. Insert flexible plastic edging in the trench so that the beaded edge is flush with the ground. Join the ends of the edging with union connectors. Anchor the edging by driving spikes every foot, using a hand sledge. Pack the soil around the edging.

5. Lay out your garden design with the plants still in their containers. As you arrange them, consider the mature sizes, bloom times and foliage textures of the plants as well as their colors.

Step C: Insert the Plants

Working with one plant at a time, use a spade or hand trowel to dig a hole twice as wide and the same depth as the plant's container. Remove the plant from the container and loosen the root ball. For large container-grown plants, use the technique for slicing through the root ball demonstrated on page 65. Place the plant in the hole and fill around it, gently patting the soil until it's compacted just enough to support the plant. Repeat with remaining plants.

Step D: Add the Mulch

Apply a 2" to 3" layer of organic mulch, such as shredded bark, shredded cypress or cocoa bean hulls, around your plants to inhibit weed growth and keep the soil moist. Water the plants thoroughly.

VARIATION: BRICK EDGING

Brick edging adds an attractive touch to garden beds, especially if you have other brick structures in your landscape. Here's an easy way to install brick edging:

1. Dig a flat-bottomed trench around the perimeter of the bed, using a flat spade. Make the trench about ½" deeper than the height of the edging material.

2. Place a ½" layer of sand in the trench and smooth it out. Place a strip of landscape fabric over the sand.

3. Lay the bricks side by side in the trench, as pictured above. Place a 2 × 4 over the bricks and tap it with a rubber mallet.

4. Spread sand over the bricks and use a broom to work the sand into the cracks.

5. Lightly mist the bricks with water to set the sand.

B. *Till amendments into the soil, then install the flexible plastic edging. Design and test the layout of the plants.*

C. *Working with one plant at a time, dig a hole twice as wide and the same depth as the container. Loosen the roots and insert each plant.*

D. *Apply a 2" to 3" layer of organic mulch over the entire bed, then water the plants thoroughly.*

Raised Garden Beds

Raised beds are attractive, functional and easy to build and maintain. Especially if your yard has poor soil, raised beds are an ideal way to add ornamental or vegetable gardens to your outdoor home. If you build a raised bed properly, fill it with high-quality topsoil and water it frequently, growing healthy plants is practically foolproof. Because these gardens are elevated, they're perfect for children as well as disabled or older family members.

In addition to their functional appeal, raised beds can serve as strong design features. They provide excellent opportunities to repeat materials used in other landscape elements. You can build raised beds from a variety of materials, including brick, cut stone, interlocking block and landscape timbers.

As you plan your raised bed, think about the types of plants you want to grow and the amount of sunlight they need. Vegetables and most flowers need 6 to 8 hours of full sun during the day. If your yard doesn't have that much sun, plant it with woodland and other shade-loving plants.

Our version of a raised bed is 5 ft. × 3 ft., 18" deep. To build this bed, you simply stack 4 × 4 cedar timbers flush on top of one another in three layers, and secure them with galvanized nails. Then you drill holes into the frame to provide drainage, which helps keep the plants healthy. Once the frame is complete, you line the bed and frame with landscape fabric to prevent weed growth and keep dirt from clogging the drainage holes. If you're planting shrubs or vegetables in your raised bed, put landscape fabric on the sides only, since these plants typically have deeper root growth than flowers.

TOOLS & MATERIALS

- Basic tools (page 16)
- Reciprocating saw
- Stakes and string
- 8-ft. 4 × 4 timbers (6)

- 6" galvanized nails
- Landscape fabric
- Galvanized roofing nails

- Topsoil
- Plantings
- Mulch
- Wood sealer protectant

3" layer of mulch

Staggered end joints

½" drainage holes

Landscape fabric

Topsoil

A. *Use a shovel to remove the grass inside the outline, then dig a trench for the first row of timbers.*

B. *Level timbers in trench, then lay the next layer, staggering the joints. Drill holes and drive nails through the holes.*

HOW TO BUILD A RAISED BED

Step A: Prepare the Site

1. Outline a 5-ft. × 3-ft. area with stakes and string to mark the location of the bed. Use a shovel to remove all of the grass or weeds inside the area.

2. Dig a flat, 2"-deep, 6"-wide trench around the perimeter of the area, just inside the stakes.

Step B: Build & Level the Base

1. Measure and mark one 54" piece and one 30" piece on each 4 × 4. Hold each timber steady on saw-horses while you cut it, using a reciprocating saw.

2. Coat each timber with a wood sealer/protectant. Let the sealer dry completely.

3. Lay the first row of the timbers in the trench. Position a level diagonally across a corner, then add or remove soil to level it. Repeat with remaining corners.

Step C: Complete the Raised Bed

1. Set the second layer of timbers in place, staggering the joints with the joint pattern in the first layer.

2. Drill ³⁄₁₆" pilot holes near the ends of the timbers; then drive in the galvanized barn nails.

3. Lay the third row of timbers, repeating the pattern of the first row to stagger the joints.

4. Drill pilot holes through the third layer, offsetting them to avoid hitting the underlying nails. Drive the nails through the pilot holes.

5. Drill ½" drainage holes, spaced every 2 ft., horizontally through the bottom layer of timbers.

TIP: PLANTING & MAINTAINING RAISED GARDEN BEDS

Raised bed gardens freeze faster and deeper than in-ground planting beds. Because the outside edges of the bed are more sensitive to temperature fluctuations, use this space for annuals and hardy perennials. Plant sensitive perennials and bulbs closer to the center, where the soil temperature is more stable.

If you live in an area with below-freezing winter temperatures, limit your plant choices to winter-hardy perennials, annual flowers and vegetables.

Raised beds also dry out faster than garden beds and require frequent waterings. Water the bed whenever the top 2" to 4" of soil is dry (depending on the depth of your bed), and before you see the soil shrink away from the sides of the bed.

6. Line the bed with strips of landscape fabric, over-lapping the strips by 6".

7. Drive galvanized roofing nails through the fabric, attaching it to the timbers.

Step D: Fill with Soil & Plants

1. Fill the bed with topsoil to within 4" of the top. Tamp the soil lightly with a shovel.

2. Add plants, loosening their root balls before planting. Apply a 3" layer of mulch, and water the plants.

C. *Place the third layer of landscape timbers over the second, staggering the joints. Secure the timbers in place with nails. Drill 1" drainage holes through the bottom row of the timbers. Line the bed with landscape fabric.*

D. *Fill the bed with topsoil, then plant your garden. Apply a 3" layer of mulch and water the garden.*

Accents

Container Gardens

Container gardens add color and texture to outdoor spaces that might otherwise look bare, such as decks, patios, stairs and pathways. With the vast array of containers and plants available, you can select arrangements to blend with any landscape style. Container gardens are also easy to create and maintain, making them ideal for those who don't have much time to spend on gardening.

Traditional container gardens combine several kinds of flowering annuals. We've created versions of two classic annual container gardens—a potted arrangement, and a moss-covered hanging basket. These arrangements are designed to add a vivid splash of color to an outdoor room without taking up a lot of space. Although we've chosen sun-loving flowering annuals, you can adapt these container gardens to grow herbs, small vegetables, spring-flowering bulbs or perennials.

Growing conditions in container gardens are different from those in a garden bed. There's a limited amount of space, and the soil dries out easily. You'll need to choose plants and soil that are compatible with this environment. Make sure the plants you buy are suitable for the container's size and can tolerate dry spells. Use a sterile potting soil mix that includes a lightweight material, such as perlite or vermiculite, to prevent the container from getting too heavy. If the potting soil doesn't contain fertilizer, you'll want to blend it with a balanced, time-release fertilizer to encourage season-long growth.

TOOLS & MATERIALS

CONTAINER:
- 12" × 5" plastic container
- Pottery shards
- Potting soil
- (A) Dark pink geranium (1)
- (B) White sweet alyssum (4)
- (C) Purple pansy (4)

HANGING BASKET:
- 12" wire hanging basket
- Dry sphagnum moss
- 2-mil landscape plastic
- Plastic food wrap
- (A) Pink ivy geranium (5)
- (B) Purple pansy (7)
- (C) Vinca major (3)

HOW TO PLANT CONTAINERS
Step A: Prepare the Container
1. Clean the container with mild soap and hot water. Rinse it thoroughly.

Planting Containers

A. *Wash the container. Open the drainage holes, and cover them with a layer of broken pottery shards.*

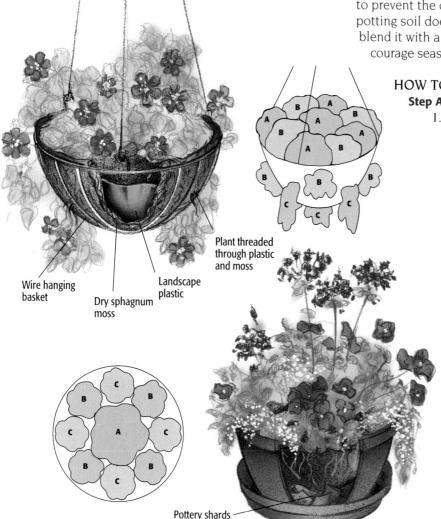

Wire hanging basket

Dry sphagnum moss

Landscape plastic

Plant threaded through plastic and moss

Pottery shards

2. Remove the plastic plugs from the drainage holes in the bottom of the container. Place pottery shards or small rocks over the drainage holes to prevent them from clogging.

Step B: Plant the Annuals

1. Leaving the plants in their containers, test-fit them in the pot to determine your final arrangement.

2. Fill the bottom of the container ⅓ full with the potting soil mix. Remove the plants from their growing containers and loosen the root balls. Arrange the plants in the pot. Backfill potting soil around the plants, leaving ½" of space at the top for watering. Water the soil thoroughly.

HOW TO MAKE A HANGING BASKET

Step A: Line the Basket

1. Cover the bottom of the wire basket with dry sphagnum moss. Tear off smaller pieces of moss and line the sides of the basket, arranging these pieces to overlap the moss on the bottom and extend to the top of the basket.

2. Measure and cut a round piece of landscape plastic to fit inside the basket. Cut X-shaped slits in the plastic where the vinca and pansies will protrude from the sides. Place the plastic over the moss, and fill the basket with potting soil up to the bottom of the slits.

Step B: Plant the Basket

1. Loosely wrap a piece of plastic wrap around each

VARIATION: CHOOSING CONTAINERS

There are many options when it comes to choosing containers, ranging from rustic wood barrels to decorative terra-cotta pots. Make sure the containers you select have drainage holes to prevent the soil from becoming waterlogged.

vinca and pansy plant. (The plastic makes it easier to pull the plants through the moss and plastic lining.) Hold each plant inside the basket and gently pull it by the stems through the plastic and the moss.

2. Carefully pull away the plastic wrap and loosen the root balls. Fill the basket halfway with potting soil.

3. Plant the geraniums and the remaining pansies inside the basket. Loosen the root ball of each plant. Backfill potting soil around the plants, leaving at least ½" of space at the top for watering.

4. Cover the spaces between the plants with pieces of sphagnum moss to help keep the soil moist between waterings. Hang the basket and water it thoroughly.

Making a Hanging Basket

B. *Fill the pot ⅓ full with soil. Test-fit the annuals. Plant the annuals, and fill the pot with soil ½" from the top.*

A. *Line the inside of the basket with pieces of dry sphagnum moss and a piece of 2-mil plastic.*

B. *Finish planting the annuals, then place pieces of moss between the plants.*

Garden ponds add interest to the landscape and provide a quiet spot for relaxing and observing nature. This elaborate pond features rushes, fish and flagstone edging.

Garden Pond Basics

Garden ponds, also called water gardens, provide a focal point in the landscape and create a feeling of serenity. Styles and features range from simple, natural-looking ponds with a few plants, to elaborate landscape features complete with fountains and submerged lights.

Garden ponds create a special place for observing nature. They're ideal for showcasing unusual aquatic plants and fish, which add interesting colors and textures. Fountains often attract birds and other wildlife to garden ponds.

Installing and maintaining a garden pond is surprisingly easy. The following information explains how to select plants and fish and outlines the basic maintenance requirements for a garden pond.

SELECTING AQUATIC PLANTS

Water gardens are ideal for aquatic plants that thrive in boggy conditions, such as water lilies and rushes. The plants grow in specially prepared containers submerged in the garden. A wide variety of aquatic plants is available at nurseries, garden centers and from mail-order suppliers. When selecting plant specimens, make sure they're compatible with your climate and the amount of sunlight that your pond will get on an average day.

ADDING AQUATIC PLANTS TO A POND

To prepare an aquatic planter, drill two 1" holes in the bottom of a container, then line it with landscape fabric. (The holes allow water to circulate past the roots of the plants, and the landscape fabric prevents the holes from getting clogged.)

Position a plant in the container and backfill around it with topsoil, leaving 2" at the top of the container. Pour a 1" layer of aquarium gravel over the soil to help keep it in place.

It's best to arrange the plants in the garden pond before adding the water. Space plants so they'll have enough room when they reach mature size. As a general rule of thumb, a garden pond should have at least one container of submerged plants for every 2 sq. ft. of pond surface; and floating plants should cover no more than ⅔ of its surface. Place taller plants, such as cattails and rushes, in the deepest area of the pond. Floating plants can be placed along the shallow edges of the liner. If your liner doesn't have a shelf, position floating plants on a stack of rocks or bricks, bringing them closer to the surface so they get enough light to thrive.

CHOOSING & ADDING FISH

Fish help support aquatic plants by supplying them with carbon dioxide. But you must keep a balance between the fish and the plants—add only one 3" fish for every 2 sq. ft. in your pond.

Make sure the fish you buy can survive in an outdoor pond. The most popular ornamental pond fish include many varieties of goldfish and brightly colored nishiki-goi, or colored carp. These fish are available at pet retailers and at some garden stores.

Do not place fish in a pond that has recently been filled with ordinary tap water—the chlorine levels will kill them. Instead, wait for the chlorine to evaporate, which takes about three days. Add only a couple of fish each day; the pond needs time to compensate for the nitrogen-rich waste the fish produce. If you add the fish all at once, they may die from excess nitrogen intake.

PROTECTING SMALL CHILDREN & ANIMALS

Young children and animals are easily enticed by the reflective quality of the water in garden ponds, and you'll need to take precautions for their safety. The best option is to install heavy wire mesh over the top of the pond. The mesh allows plants to grow through the holes, and it can be removed once the children are older.

PREPARING FOR WINTER

Unless you live in a Zone 9 or 10 region, you'll need to prepare your pond for the winter between mid and late fall. If you live in Zones 5 to 8, you can leave plants and fish in the pond, but you'll need to keep it from freezing over completely. If you live in Zones 1 to 4, bring all plants and fish indoors and drain the pond. Prune the plant stems down to 1", and leave them in a dry, dark location. Keep the fish in an aerated aquarium filled with 3-day-old tap water.

SAFETY TIP:

Protect young children and animals by covering the surface of the pond with heavy wire mesh. The mesh is discreet; the plants grow through the holes, camouflaging the mesh. Never leave young children unsupervised near water.

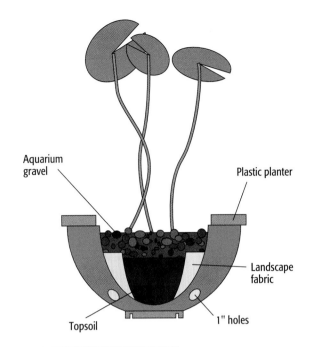

Aquarium gravel

Plastic planter

Landscape fabric

Topsoil

1" holes

(left) Garden ponds are a delicate ecosystem. Be careful to keep the proper balance of plants and fish. Allow no more than ⅔ of the pond's surface to be covered by floating plants, and have only one 3" fish for every 2 sq. ft. of water.

(below) This water garden showcases the unusual colors and textures of goldfish, lily pads and lotus flowers.

Accents

Garden Ponds

The simplest way to build a garden pond is to use a prefabricated pond liner. These easy-to-use liners, available at home centers and garden shops, come in a variety of shapes and sizes.

Most pond liners are made from PVC, rubber or fiberglass. We've chosen a fiberglass pond liner, primarily because fiberglass is more durable than a PVC liner and less expensive than rubber. If you live in an area with exceptionally cold winters, use a rubber liner instead; fiberglass can crack if it's exposed to severely cold weather for prolonged periods.

To give the pond a more natural appearance, we set coping stones around the perimeter. When you're adding coping stones, don't place them over the edges of the liner—the weight of the stones can weaken and crack it.

Select the site for your garden pond carefully. A low-lying, level area provides the most natural setting, and requires far less digging than a sloped site. Ponds should not receive too much direct sunshine, however, so choose a location that is shaded for at least half the day. Do not build your pond directly under a tree—you can easily damage the tree's roots during excavation, and bacteria from fallen leaves can contaminate the pond's water.

If you're going to stock the pond with fish or delicate plants, let the water sit for at least three days before you add them, to give the chlorine time to evaporate.

TOOLS & MATERIALS

- Basic tools (page 16)
- Rope
- Fiberglass pond liner
- Long 2 × 4
- Sand
- Flagstone coping stones
- Dry mortar mix

HOW TO INSTALL A GARDEN POND

Step A: Outline the Pond

1. Set the fiberglass liner in place. Outline the base of the liner, using a rope.
2. Hold a level perpendicular against the outside edge, and use it as a guide to outline the perimeter of the liner.

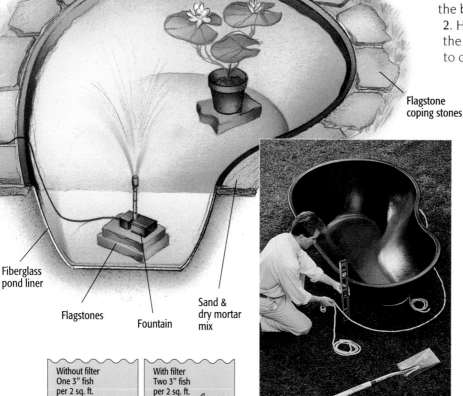

Fiberglass pond liner

Flagstones
Fountain
Sand & dry mortar mix

Flagstone coping stones

Without filter
One 3" fish per 2 sq. ft.

With filter
Two 3" fish per 2 sq. ft.

A. *Set the liner in place. Carefully outline both the base and the outside edges of the liner, using ropes.*

B. *Excavate the site for the liner, sloping the sides toward the center. Test-fit the liner, adjusting the hole until the liner fits.*

Step B: Excavate the Site

1. Measure the depth of the liner at the center. Excavate the base area to this depth. Dig out the remaining part of the outlined area, sloping the sides toward the flat bottom. Make this area as deep as necessary to hold the edges of the liner slightly above ground level.

2. Test-fit the shell repeatedly, digging and filling areas until the shape of the hole matches the shell.

Step C: Level the Liner

Remove any rocks or sharp objects remaining in the excavated site, then set the liner into the hole. Check the liner for level, and adjust as necessary.

Step D: Fill the Pond & Excavate for the Edging

1. Begin slowly filling the liner. As the water level rises, pack wet sand into the gaps between the shell and the sides of the hole.

2. Dig a shallow trench around the perimeter of the liner, wide enough to hold the stones.

Step E: Set the Coping Stones

1. Spread a mixture of 20 parts sand to one part dry mortar evenly in the trench. Lightly spray the sand mixture with water.

2. Fit the stones together in the trench, placing them so they don't touch the edges of the liner. Create an overflow point for excess water by setting one of the stones ½" lower than the others.

VARIATION: INSTALLING A FOUNTAIN

Fountains help promote healthy plants and fish by circulating the water through a submersible pump. There are many affordable, easy-to-install models available at home centers and garden supply stores.

Install the fountain before you fill the pond. Lay a 2 × 4 across the top of the pond to mark where the water level will be when the pond is filled. Place the pump on a stack of rocks or bricks in the center of the pond, then attach the riser and fountain head, according to the manufacturer's directions. Adjust the riser height so the fountain head stands just above the top of the board.

After you've filled the pond, turn the fountain on and observe the height of the spray. If you'd like to adjust the spray height, unplug the pump and make adjustments by turning the restrictor valve on the fountain head.

C. Remove any rocks from the hole, and set the liner in place. Adjust the hole until the edges are slightly above ground level.

D. Begin filling the liner slowly with water. Pack wet sand into any gaps between the liner and the ground.

E. Dig a shallow trench around the liner. Line the trench with a sand and dry mortar mix, and set the stones.

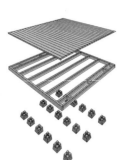

Contributors

WE WOULD LIKE TO THANK THE FOLLOWING COMPANIES
FOR THEIR CONTRIBUTIONS TO THIS BOOK:

Tad Anderson Landscape Design
Studio: P.O. Box 5264
Minnetonka, MN 55343-2264
(612) 473-8387

Bachman's Landscaping Service
6010 Lyndale Avenue South
Minneapolis, MN 55419
(612) 861-7600

Black & Decker (U.S.) Inc.
701 East Joppa Road
Townson, MD 21286
(800) 544-6986

DEKBRANDS, Inc.
(Manufacturer of DEK-Block Piers)
P.O. Box 14808
Minneapolis, MN 55414
(612) 331-4755
Technical Support: (800) 664-2705

Exterior Design Studio
5012 Benton Avenue
Edina, MN 55436
(612) 922-4445

GreenTech
1300 Oakside Circle
Chanhassen, MN 55317
(612) 368-3151

Hedberg Aggregates
1205 Nathan Lane North
Plymouth, MN 55441
(612) 512-2849

Interlock Concrete Products
3535 Bluff Drive
Jordan, MN 55352-8302
(612) 492-3636

Minnesota Valley Landscape, Inc.
14505 Johnson Memorial Drive
Shakopee, MN 55379
(612) 445-4004

Rain Bird Sprinkler Mfg. Corp.
7590 Britannia Court
San Diego, CA 92713-3407
Sales: (800) 435-5672
Expert Advice: (800) 724-6247

The Toro Company
(Manufacturer of Low-voltage Lighting)
8111 Lyndale Avenue South
Bloomington, MN 55420-1196
(800) 595-6841

Weber Horticultural Design
P.O. Box 5264
Minnetonka, MN 55343-2264
(612) 473-8387

THE FOLLOWING BOOKS AND MAGAZINES PROVIDE HELPFUL INFORMATION ON LANDSCAPING AND GARDENING:

Backyard Design: Making the Most of the Space Around Your House
By Jean Spiro Breskend
Bullfinch Press

The Complete Guide to Home Plumbing
Black & Decker Home
Improvement Library
Creative Publishing international

The Complete Guide to Home Wiring
Black & Decker Home
Improvement Library
Creative Publishing international

Designing Your Outdoor Home
Black & Decker Outdoor Home Library
Creative Publishing international

The Family Handyman (Magazine)
Home Service Publications, Inc.

Fine Gardening (Magazine)
The Taunton Press, Inc.

Garden Gate: The Illustrated Guide to Home Gardening and Design (Magazine)

Today's Homeowner (Magazine)
Times-Mirror Magazines

Landscape Design & Construction
Black & Decker
Home Improvement Library
Creative Publishing international

Landscaping From the Ground Up
By Sara Jane von Trapp
Taunton Books & Video

The Outdoor Room
By David Stevens
Random House

Outdoor Wood Furnishings
Black & Decker Outdoor Home Library
Creative Publishing international

A Portfolio of Water Garden & Specialty Landscape Ideas
Creative Publishing international

Today's Homeowner: Around the Yard
Creative Publishing international

Watering Systems for Lawn & Garden: A Do-It-Yourself Guide
By R. Dodge Woodson
Storey Publishing

PHOTO CREDITS:

Photographers:
©Walter Chandoha: page 106
©Crandall & Crandall: page 28a
©Crandall & Crandall/Rogers Gardens:
page 53d
©David Hamsley: page 105
©Saxon Holt: pages 7, 53a, 61c
©Mark A. Madsen: page 5
©Charles Mann: pages 61d, 96-97, 107b

©Jerry Pavia: pages 29c, 29e, 77a, 107a
©Angie Spann: page 61a
©Michael S. Thompson: page 29a

Manufacturers:
Anderson Design Services, Ltd.: page 83a
Bachman's Landscaping Service: page 52
Intermatic Incorporated: pages 53b, 53c

Index